PENGUIN BOOKS

THE COMPLETE GOLF GAMESMANSHIP

Stephen Potter was born in 1900 and educated at West-
minster School and Merton College, Oxford, where he
read English. In 1926 he became a lecturer in English at
London University, and in 1938 he joined the staff of the
B.B.C. as a writer-producer. There he became editor of the
literary features and poetry, and in 1943 Chairman of the
Literary Committee. His principal programmes were the
'How' series (with Joyce Grenfell) and Professional Por-
traits, and he was originator and editor of the New Judge-
ment series. He has been dramatic critic of the *New States-
man*, book critic of the *News Chronicle* and editor of the
Leader Magazine. His other books include *D. H. Lawrence*
(1930), *The Nonesuch Coleridge* (1934), *Minnow among
Tritons: Letters of Mrs S. T. Coleridge* (1934), *Potter on
America* (1956), *Steps to Immaturity* (1959), *Anti-Woo*
(1965), *The Complete Golf Gamesmanship* (1968) and
Pedigree: The Evolution of English Native Words (1968).
His anthology of English humour, *The Sense of Humour*,
is also available in Penguins. Stephen Potter died in 1971.

THE COMPLETE

GOLF GAMESMANSHIP

*

STEPHEN POTTER

*

ILLUSTRATED BY LT.-COL.
FRANK WILSON

PENGUIN BOOKS

Penguin Books Ltd, Harmondsworth, Middlesex, England
Penguin Books Australia Ltd, Ringwood, Victoria, Australia

—

First published by William Heinemann 1968
Published in Penguin Books 1971

—

Copyright © The Estate of Stephen Potter, 1968

—

Made and printed in Great Britain
by Richard Clay (The Chaucer Press), Ltd,
Bungay, Suffolk
Set in Linotype Baskerville

In memoriam

Edgar Lansbury (9)
Ronald Simpson (11)

ACKNOWLEDGEMENTS

I OWE a considerable debt, in these pages, to the golf books of Herbert Warren Wind, and to such worthy successors of the great Bernard Darwin, in the field of Golf Correspondents (which seems to breed good writing) as Mr Ward-Thomas. More directly I am grateful to three friends who are not only great games-men but who also happen to be considerable players of the game. To Alistair Cooke, that is, for advice and suggestions; to Geoff Paine, for many suggestions, for basic ploys and gambits, and for deep-seated surgical corrections of the kind of errors which were more obvious to him than to one who was never actually once Plus Two; and to Henry Longhurst, not only for a few of the more sophisticated ploys, recorded here, but for the pleasure he gives to all golfers by his articles and television commentaries.

CONTENTS

CONTENTS

CONTENTS

the players are in close contact

I

WHY CHOOSE GOLF?

WHY has no book been dedicated to the gamesmanship of golf? This question must have been asked again and again, even if one has not actually heard it. What must be the answer? Is it not because, so long as one is still playing golf, one* is reluctant to reveal the essential secrets? But the Great Handicapper calls. My debts to a great game must be paid, the small monument must be completed.

Which game is the best of all of them? The large majority of those with the widest experience will say golf. Why? Partly because it is the most complicated. No two shots, even with the same club at the same hole, are identical. But surely the same applies to polo, where the shots are actually played one-handed on a moving ball from a moving object, on which only three men in a thousand are able to stay seated.

* For 'one' read 'I' throughout.

Yes, but what gives to golf its depths, its flavour, its feel which makes us think we are not playing the game but living it, is the richness of its gamesmanship.

I once wrote that golf was the gamesgame of gamesgames. At the time I was under the influence of James Joyce. But the fact is that when *Gamesmanship* made its first tentative appearance, golf was the setting chosen for many of the first crude experiments; and it was found that of all games golf was the most susceptible to gamesmanship for two reasons. First, it is a still ball game ('the less violent physically, the more vulnerable psychologically'). Secondly, the players are in close contact ('the smaller the orbit the more potent the ploy'). A well-timed failure to smile at an opponent's joke or to react to his sporting gesture is ineffective if the two of you are separated by the length of a tennis court.

Golf gamesmanship is still in an early stage. As golf spreads from Lisbon to Lithuania, from the seaboards of the Pacific coast line to the permafrost of Northern Finland, the gambits of new peoples, deep bedded in their religion and culture, must be recorded and analysed: for 'unless ye know them, they are not known'. Such developments as driving ranges and par 3 courses and putting in the home are too raw, as yet, to have acquired an offensive–defensive psychology: but all these, with golf watching, and TV watching of golf watching well to the fore, are already establishing their place in the richest and most varied of gamesmanship's many fields.

2

HISTORICAL OUTLINE

GAMBITOUS NATURE OF HISTORY

HISTORY is a gambit. More precisely the writing of history is a double or treble gambit. It is a way of saying 'I think' and 'what about this' in a tone which is supposed, simply by adding the word 'History', to silence argument.

It is also a way of saying 'Nothing surprises *me* because it's all happened before, if not more so.' It is a method therefore of making recent events seem a good deal less remarkable than people who have the temerity to write about recent events would lead us to suppose.

Take the moderately recent date of 1953. In this year Hogan, not long recovered from a grave accident, won, at Carnoustie, one of the most difficult courses in the world, his first British Open with a last round of 68. Scotland is unlikely to forget this round, just as the English are unlikely to forget Cotton's 65 at Sandwich in the Open of 1934, which helped him to break American domination, and they will point out that for that 65 he was limited to the techniques and equipment of a former generation.

But nothing is history proof. History can take both those scores and put them in their place by stating – not suggesting – that Ouimet or Vardon, to say nothing of Tom Morris junior, could, given today's balls, clubs, fairways and greens and the peace of mind engendered by endorsement contracts, have beaten both those scores by three strokes or better.

More sophisticated is the use of the atmosphere of history to blunt the vigour of an athletic but unbookish young opponent. Encyclopaedias and museums can sap, in junior players, the desire to win. If a youth can be made to feel that his match with you is part of a Nordic ritual which has been going on for centuries, it may act as a depressant. The encyclopaedic approach ('first played in 4th century Alexandria'), could dilute, however slightly, the spirit of attack if this fact is first mentioned in a gloomy changing room. Say 'Apparently Aubrey writes of "the games of clout and blatherball" – this would be about 1656'. Say this if guest is expecting to be offered a drink. Pictures of Dutch burghers forcing a quoit or disk to slide on ice can make even a scratch player feel momentarily as if he were floundering about in historical gravy. 'Curious old print' you can suddenly say to your opponent, in the afternoon round.

DOES GOLF MEAN GOLF?

Before we leave these preliminaries it is worth remembering that it may come in useful if we learn some patter about the origin of the word golf:

PHILOLOGIST (15 handicap): It's really the same as German *kolbe* – *kólfr* in Old Norse.

PHILOLOGICAL BOOB (7): Excuse me?

PHIL: Norse. Old Norwegian.

P.B. (*after long pause*): What, you don't mean sort of Vikings? ... you don't mean they played –

PHIL: No no. No no no no. The word 'golf' originally meant *club*.

P.B.: Golf Clubs are quite old places, then?

PHIL: Not Club – club.

P.B.: I see – then what does Club come from?

Philologist may have to change subject, and it is certainly only a trivial ploy. But it can affect concentration in the middle of a game and, although I am keen on a derivation myself, it is in general a powerful conversation-stopper, especially with women, who though attracted to men able to speak Spanish and modern Greek, consider philology unsexy. Women do, however, pay slight, if off-hand, attention to pronunciation. And here the twelve principal ways of saying the word 'golf' itself is quite a good rallying point.

'No, no', begin. 'It's what *you say* that counts. There is no "right" way to pronounce the word.'

'Do you mean I'm saying it wrong?'

'It's all a question of usage.'

Note. Only highly trained gamesmen should attempt advanced ploys of this nature: and to make a good job of this particular approach, some seemingly genuine knowledge is required. This analysis of a few of the pronunciations of the word 'golf' may be useful:

gŏlf: English and absolutely ordinary, if one likes the absolutely ordinary.

gŏff: English 'upper-class' or O.K. pronunciation, 1890–1950.

gŏl-f: England. Refined ladies who do not actually play.

gerlf: Fairly well-bred ladies who are tremendously keen.

gerf: Aggressively well-bred country ladies.

geaiorlf: West London cockney – a rare sound and becoming rarer.

gorf: The new cockney.

gōlf: Quite common but totally inexplicable.

gor: 'Strine' (Australian) as in phrase 'plygor' ('play golf'. Datum kindly supplied by Afferbeck Lauder).

gouf: Lowland Scots who wish to preserve accent. Recommended for Scottish Nationalist candidates.

garlf: Northern Idaho.

göff

gerlf

SCOTSMANSHIP AND EARLY GOLF PLAY

The history of golf gamesmanship must, we all warmly admit, start with Scotland.

There is no doubt that the basic Scotch gambits and the atmosphere of Scottish golf play were created as if by Nature for gamesmanship. First there is the ploy of the abundance of tremendous old characters. Idiosyncrasies flourish as the square of the number of stones per agricultural acre: and in early golf here it soon became established that unless you were, or at any rate knew personally, a famous old character, the situation was one-down. Somebody called something like Auld

Reikie, or, more simply, Tom, must be known to say good morning to you and if possible add a word of sour advice, with musical comedy Scots' phrases like:

'My! but yon was a lucky yin.'

'Bad played, didna desairve it.'

But perhaps the main corner-stone of Scotsmanship is the Spartan ploy, which implies the necessity, in order to qualify for full membership, of running the gauntlet of physical discomfort or pain. In terms of golf, this means that top golf is impossible without top discomfort. Read carefully this description from the Badminton Library *Golf*, of a match in 1870:

Curiously enough he was unable to use a cleek for the bad lying putt. These he negotiated with his iron.

No mention of the peculiar state of the grass. No word about bad greenkeeping. That would have been, in Scotland, ungamesmanlike.

Another Scotsmanlike attitude which pervaded golf is the belief in the necessity of the essential home-madeness of everything. At St Andrew's in particular one could or should have known personally the ball-maker. When the carved wooden heads of the earlier clubs went out and iron heads were substituted, though it was not necessary actually to forge these heads oneself, it was required form to know the famous old character concerned, and if possible to stand in his smithy and see the sparks fly. It was correct to say, with a touch of Scots in your own voice:

'Ay, it was a gran' sight to see the sparks flyin'.*

* It would seem to be impossible to suggest, nowadays, an association with club making. But nothing was impossible to Douglas Ackminster. Not only did he carry a small stick of synthetic bitumen with which he deftly repaired any club grip which was becoming unstuck: he even suggested that he had worked in

NEANDERTHAL GAMESMANSHIP

To historians of gamesmanship, the great interest of this period is in the primitive simplicity of the moves in the battle, often too physically rough to qualify as gamesmanship. There are records of 'scrambling and

wrangling for precedence on the first tee'. If one was held up by the foursome ahead, it was not sufficient, in the Scotland of that time, to stand with one hand on the hip and look pained. It was a 'question of thrust and attack'. 'It often happens that in their burning anxiety to get past, one of the quick party sends his ball into a bunker. Whereupon the slow party rallies, and there is a neck and neck race for the putting green.'

Then, suddenly, in the midst of the old savagery, there is a glimpse of something more subtle.

'Do not stand close enough to your opponent to annoy him, and do not stand "behind his eye" as it is called ... *If he be a nervous player, find out where he prefers you to stand.*'

---

a factory for making steel shafts. But he went too far when he mentioned the hours six to six, and hinted that he was one of the last victims of the exploitation of child labour.

WORK OF HORACE HUTCHINSON

That line (our italics) was probably written in 1889 – yet what a mature and even sophisticated grasp of gamesmanship it implies. Where do these quotations come from? From Horace G. Hutchinson, certainly the man who came nearest to the comprehension of golf gamesmanship before its first naming. Read Hutchinson on the question of rule breaking, of lightly touching the sand with the club head in the bunker, of causing the ball to move. Nowadays we know well, if opponent so errs, to say 'bad luck' in a dead sort of Soames Forsyte voice, in other words 'Sorry, we saw'. But in those days Opponent might easily have said, 'Do you want me to count that?' Difficult, in that case, to exact the penalty. Impossible if opponent was a female.

But there is something fascinating about the simplicity of these earlier ploys. One feels, almost, a touch of envy. 'Of all delinquents against the unwritten code,' says Hutchinson elsewhere, and the gamesman pricks up his ears, 'the grossest offender is perhaps he who stands over you, with triumph spiced with derision, as you labour in a bunker, and aggressively counts your score aloud.' Neanderthal gamesmanship no doubt – but note, behind that remark, the quickening pulse of the born analyst of the human motive, the careful student of human ethology, the gamesman.

COMING OF THE ENGLISH

There is no doubt that in the realm of Golf, England is, historically, a one-down nation. To begin with it was to Scotland: and then, after a brief interval of power, it was to America.

Scotland hung on to its rights as Father of all aspects of the game and has still maintained its position as the Moses of golf, dealing with rules and commandments. (To those sensitive to such things it is obvious that Moses, at 14 handicap, would be a tough opponent in a 4-ball.) A very late nineteenth-century Scot could write (1890) that 'the history of the Scotch game, in foreign parts, England, France, India, Canada, Texas, need not delay us long'.

What could England do? Its development of the closed, inland course diminished rather than improved the possibilities of gamemanship. Sheep on the fairways, droppings on the green, courting couples in the rough are problems invented and developed for the links of Scotland.

TWO CHARACTERS

What England did do was to develop the new atmosphere of the gentlemanly club-house, and much later, the ladies wing, starting point of the L.G.U. (Ladies Gamesmanship Union). More important was the development of two characters, different, but both typical. H. Vardon was thought of as typically English not only because he was English but because he was noted for swing, style, gentlemanliness and the right clothes, including especially a Norfolk jacket.* Side by side with Vardon was the still more English Englishman, J. H. Taylor, who yet somehow managed to out-Scot the Scotch at their own gambit. He must have been a famous Old Character almost from the cradle, being short and strong and chin-jutting and with flat peaked cap and a golf style which looked all utility and strength, but was in fact composed of art and determination. Vardon's triumph was to master the Open by style, and look the part; whereas Taylor's was to win it almost as frequently by strength, ordinariness, pluck and determination, and to play that role to perfection.

Early Lost Ball Play ('I think you've got more chance of finding it over here.')

But the gambits were unconscious. Gamesmanship played little part. This is the realm of pure good play – something which leaves altogether too pleasant a taste in the mouth to be included in this book.

* It is not true, as was once thought, that he never took this off.

U.S.A. AND THE COMING OF
BLACK AND WHITE SHOES

Soon after the beginning of this century, an American won the British Amateur.

The beginnings of U.S. golf might have been deliberately planned to emphasize the overwhelming nature of this event. In America the game started *extremely late* and to begin with *feebly*. The first American golf shot was played at five minutes past ten on 4 March 1889. By the end of the year there were twelve golfers. In 1890 this number was increased by one. The 'Apple Tree Gang' was so called because they laid out 6 holes in an orchard, which was increased in 1894 to 9.

Note the careful build up to Mr Travis's achievement. All unaware, Britain was taking its first rash steps towards the almost insuperably one-down position of a Goliath. No wonder that within ten years of these stone-age events any American invader, his club heads fashioned from the naked flint, assumed the psychological dimensions of a David. No wonder that in the brief noon of British supremacy, a small shadow seemed to move across the sun. In the year 1904 the amateur championship was played at Sandwich. On the first tee, W. J. Travis, a distinguished golfer in his own country, an Amateur Champion, perhaps the greatest putter of his time, had enjoyed the hospitality of golfers during a previous visit to this country. But on this occasion, he not only won the game but the gamesmanship.

What went wrong? *Faulty warm-hearted play*. Bleak reception, failure of hosts to introduce American competitors to the Sandwich Club, no locker for Mr Travis,

who had to change in a sort of passage, in a draughty
corner which now bears, on a plaque in the wall,
modelled in ebony, a pair of crossed golf clubs re-
versed. Distinguished American visitors enter Club-
house by side entrances. Bleak sea winds on unshel-
tered course.

Mr Travis won. His feelings were recorded. Quite
soon vast improvements were seen in the reception of
American visitors. They were allowed to take meals
within one mile of the club-house, and indeed slightly
nearer. Even at Sandwich, for the Walker Cup match
of 1967, it was noticed that in the long queues for the
sausage roll and beer tent, and for the lavatory, there
was no discrimination between English and American
spectators.

Why does Travis's name stand so high in the list of
American gamesmen? To what extent was it deliberate? Did he say he had never heard of Sandwich, and
did he purposely refuse to have dinner with somebody
somewhere? And did he and his friends deliberately
entertain, in the States, the year before, a group of
Oxford and Cambridge players in order that he should
be 'barely recognized' by two of them at Sandwich who
had given what, though it seemed to Oxford and Cambridge no doubt an embarrassingly effusive greeting,
inevitably seemed to Travis to be a 'perfunctory wave'?

Whatever the truth, no chance, no possible chance,
now in 1968, of perfunctory waves in Britain to visiting
American stars. In my own Club, scarcely a stronghold
of broad-minded democracy, I noticed last month that
there is now a special changing room set aside for visitors of any race or creed, and it is considerably more
polished up than the adjoining quarters for regular
members. Looking back, we must all acknowledge the

success of Travis's Offended Ploy, and accept this classic success in the field of international gamesmanship.*

Glance of a Gamesman

Travis may have been a shade too mature and prickly to be perfectly fitted for the part of the youthful challenger. Besides, the ideal David needs the ideal Goliath. This was provided in the celebrated 1913 American Open at Brookline when Vardon and Ray were beaten in the play-off by Francis Ouimet. Vardon was a great and celebrated British champion but was too gentle and gentlemanly to be a Goliath. Ted Ray, on the other hand, was large and strong and hit the ball so hard that the ground seemed to thunder under his feet, although both of them were off the ground at the moment of impact. Ouimet was the David of sporting history because he fulfilled the following requirements. He

 looked slender
 looked gentle
 was naturally sporting
 was young
 was a gentleman but

* Britain made one wishy-washy attempt to find a counter to the Travis ploy, but it was too long delayed to make its impact. Travis was the first player to use a Schenectady putter in this country. After a pause of 8 years it was banned by the R. & A.

had poor parents
who were uninterested in golf
and didn't encourage him to play.

In the triple play-off with Vardon, Ted Ray, the strong and nerveless man, faded away first. He had no resilience, no reserves of gamesmanship. With great courage, he only lost by 7 strokes.

KING GAMESMAN

It was the beginning of the Great One-down-ness of British Golf. After the war, for a year or two, we carried on with extraordinary bravery. But the final capture of golf supremacy was achieved by a man who was neither a David nor a Goliath. He was the first man to wear in England black and white golf shoes, a man who in the whole history of gamesmanship, was probably second in skill only to the great Doctor, to W. G. Grace himself.

In Ouimet it was unconscious. In the case of Walter Hagen, even if his most successful moves were not always the result of planning, it was an art which he himself helped to create.

He was born with it. Hagen started as a 'natural games player', which in the U.S. can mean that he was also good at baseball. Hagen was actually playing in Ouimet's Championship, but few had heard of him. Incredibly, he was rather difficult to notice. Yet in the twenties, even and especially in Britain, Hagen became the biggest gamesname in golf.

The first impact of Hagen struck us before I was fully alert to the possibilities of golf. A visiting American golfer, I read, on the way over, had practised by 'driving golf-balls into the sea from the deck of the

Mauretania'. Later, he 'loosened up with iron shots into the Thames from the roof of the Savoy Hotel'. It all happened a decade or so before the principles of gamesmanship were properly settled in my mind. 'Typical,' I said. I was prone to find things 'typical'. Hagen was 'showy'. We liked our professionals to be quiet and quietly clothed, salt of the earth and with a way of calling you 'sir' which meant that we were all free men but shared a sense of degree, priority and place. We did not mind, we rather liked it if the dark

flannel trousers of our professionals were a little mud-died round the turn-ups. We were quite prepared to allow them into our changing-rooms, and indeed into the front door porches of their own clubs. And here was Hagen, perfectly polite, but without a touch of deference. Immediately after '14–'18, the British were still feeling that they were as pleased with Ouimet's victory as the Americans had been. But now was the time to get things back to normal. A young generation of British stars was represented by Duncan the Scot and Abe Mitchell the strong and silent Englishman. Even Duncan had remodelled his swing under the spell of Vardon, so that when he won the first post-war British Open in 1920, it was regarded as a particularly British return to normal. Hagen, a young over-dressed American, paying his first visit to this country, aroused some head-shaking sympathy in that championship by taking over 80 for every single round. Although he himself had two championships already to his credit, they were both American. So that was American golf.

Next year, 1921, it is true that for the first time the Cup went to the States: but it was to Jock Hutchinson, till so recently a Scot of Scots, and still basically a St Andrew's man, who, moreover, finished level with an English amateur, R. H. Wethered. He was lucky to beat him in the play-off since Wethered manipulated a remarkably advanced gamesmanship ploy – he 'didn't want to stay up because he had promised to play in a cricket match in England that Saturday morning'. In 1922 things had settled down again for good, surely, Havers calmly refusing to crack under foreign pressure. It was this Havers who did so well later at Moor Park by acquiring the silver hair and presence of a Benedictine abbot. Abe Mitchell, country squire to the last, never accepted stroke play. He would have agreed that medal play 'was little better than rifle practice'.

But the year of the gamesman was at hand, and for Britain it was Hagen, in 1922. He was to win our Open four times. I do not say that he ever won entirely by gamesmanship. To be winner of the U.S. P.G.A. in four successive years showed that he had a thread of skill as well. But I do say that had our small manuals of the gamesman's art existed at that date, his success could have been partly countered. And what were his chief gambits? There was of course the majestic use of clothesmanship, which is in essence the art of looking the opposite of the Opposition – the shoes, and the plus fours which were almost plus sixes – the butterfly among the drones. Let me mention also his famous last-minuting, his strolling on to the first tee with 30 seconds to spare, and, on occasions when this would not bring disqualification, using his ability to keep his opponent waiting 40 minutes on the first tee at the beginning of a 72-hole match.

There were counterploys, even then. The great Englishman, Archie Compston, was perfectly capable of a gamesmanship counter. He was no mean clothesman himself, though he concentrated on the rough tweeds and the loosely knotted scarf approach. He was large and leonine. He could keep waiting the man who kept everybody waiting: and in one famous 72-hole match, he beat Hagen 18 up and 17 to play.

The very size of this disaster suggests that a gamesman is involved. If the defeat is big enough one is inclined to dismiss it. The victim is 'off colour', or is suffering from some excess. (In ordinary Club play it is possible, by suggesting that 'Somebody has a very generous handicap', to have the winner pretty well sent to Coventry.) Be this as it may, just before the coup de grace in the Compston/Hagen match, Hagen paused by the pond to the left of the 15th green on the High Course at Moor Park, sat on his haunches and stared at the water. 'Marvellous, isn't it?' he said. He was looking at the tadpoles.

It was when he was fighting against odds in a close match that Hagen was at his best. Bernard Darwin describes the occasion when, having driven his ball deep into a wood, he had the crowd moved back as if he intended to come out sideways and then 'as if suddenly spying a loophole of escape, played a magnificent iron shot through a gap in the trees right on to the green. His opponent was finished.'

Hagen is my first choice among living gamesmen. By such touches, finely conceived in themselves, he built up a character in which gamesmanship grew naturally, and to which gamesmanship was naturally credited. I remember as if it were yesterday – it must have been 40 years ago – reading a report in *The Times*, by Bernard Darwin, of Hagen in play and finding his ball lodged against a boundary post on the left of the course. 'Without pausing for a moment' (I am quoting from memory) 'he took out of his bag, like a conjuror producing a rabbit out of his hat, a left-handed club, with which he knocked the ball 150 yards down the fairway ...' In the days when a golfer could carry round thirty clubs if he wanted to, I guess that a left-handed club was a fairly normal addition. But such was the power of Hagen that he was able, I have no doubt, to suggest that this notion was invented by himself. Impossible stories were told, most of them mythical. It was said that, not having been to bed the night before, he once arrived for an important match, and played it, in a dinner jacket. Untrue; but when it was said that as Captain of his Ryder Cup team he somehow outdiddled or flummoxed the opposition – well, the truth of that is that Hagen was Hagen, a mixture, it has been said, of the man who was blessed with strength and shrewdness, and who could at the same time enjoy the appearance of being the most carefree and happy-go-lucky character in the world.

BOB JONESISM

Perhaps we are too close to the later history of this subject to see its developments clearly. At the end of the twenties Hagen was of course eclipsed by Mr Robert Jones, who, for all his brilliance in golf has always been a disappointment in the world of golf gamesmanship. Many heads are shaken when his name comes up. Pure play and unquestioned excellence is the death of technique. Against the bravest opposition, merit and sportsmanship emasculates the gambit and nullifies the ploy.

GAMBIT OF HENRY COTTON

Through the twenties and thirties, England and America exchanged gamesmanship techniques. For a time – and on almost all team occasions – England faded. We bred excellent golf gamesmen within our own walls, including charmers of the old school, hard luck men, regular guys and infant prodigies. All played their parts. One restored our prestige. Few will immediately agree with me that the most successful as a golfer, Henry Cotton, was also the most successful as a gamesman. But the Cotton gambit was a powerful one, as useful in life as it is in golf. No Unnecessary Smiling, as we might name it, is as effective as it is simple. Suddenly there was a man on our golf courses who looked serious, who looked as if he meant it, who was going to take the nonsense out of 'only a game'. One can dance mad boleros as soon as one is in the changing room; but Not Smiling within the boundaries of the actual course is a powerful weapon. Not smiling on the green or on the tee. Not smiling when held up. Not even smiling when watching another match.

Not smiling is something totally different from looking displeased. It suggests single mindedness and concentration. It was interesting to watch Cotton *v.* Alf Padgham. It was only at his peak that Padgham was able to counter-establish his more immediately attractive approach of easy chat which sometimes included a remark to the crowd. Or there was Cotton *v.* Dai Rees, who, equally determined, had to live up to the gambit of Volatile Welshman invented for him by the head-line writers.

How was Cotton so successful? Remember that besides the discipline of his expression there were no untidy ends about his appearance, his personality or his game. His trousers were no well less cut than his head and his hair. For clothes and general appearance he did for English professionalism what Hagen did for American. He not only accepted Hagen's black and white outfit, he improved on it.

When at last Cotton broke through, and won his first Open at Sandwich in 1936, I followed him on his last round. It was a tricky one. In the end, in spite of Cotton's big lead, the man who came second was only two strokes behind. At last Cotton drove straight down the 72nd fairway and the crowd started to clap as they all speeded to the last green. At this point a development took place, which has since been the subject of endless argument between historians. Cotton, realizing he had won, smiled *although still in play*.

Let me add one more unrecorded footnote to history. Who *did* come second? A slender youth with a willowy swing. In the years to come he was to develop into no mean non-smiler himself, and although he hadn't quite the profile, he was not less effective, so far as the winning of the British Open was concerned. His name was A. D. Locke.*

Every reader will know his name Non-Smilers in the ranks of his own Club and will be able to judge their effectiveness for himself. If one can establish a non-smiling position in life it is possible, provided one has the right kind of nose, to force people to stare at one's

* 'Not Locke but Brews was second. Another typical memory failure.' G. Boyce.

face, with a sort of petrified hope, a plea for some sign. But profiles are important in this gambit, although a few Television personalities have done remarkably

Ineffective Non-Smiler

well, as non-smilers, without any profile to speak of whatever.

Let me add as a point of important recent golf gamesmanship history that since the War the United States has developed its own brand of poised profile, its own 'O.K. names', to use a useful phrase from lifemanship, its own O.K. golf courses.

So far as U.S. *v.* G.B. is concerned, Britain, in default of improved play, must concentrate on its own position as Great Originator, and its special ploys of 'Stand aside for history', Honourable Companies, Royal Clubs and ancient dignity strongly lashed with hallowed turf and imperishable scenes. Not for British clubs, we let it be known, such frivolous luxuries as private cinemas, thousand dollar subscriptions and heated swimming pools on the very margin of the course. But even here Britain's natural superiority is being seriously threatened by America, where a different time scale causes turf to become hallowed at a rattling speed.

No institution emphasizes this better than the Masters tournament at Augusta, Georgia. When I first saw this course some years ago, my wife and I were shown round by the Secretary who in manner had the gravity and charm of a youthful college Provost or Warden. He probably was one. We were shown the house of Mr Jones, the summer residence of President Eisenhower – small, white unpretentious. Inside the simple colonial type club-house Mr Jones's original golf clubs were on display. No formality or fuss: yet somehow it is Number One.

If the U.S.G.A. is one up over every other organization in America, then Augusta is two up. How is it done? By the presence of Mr Jones? By no means entirely. *The Executive Chairman is the master games-man of all time,* if I may quote the private comment of Henry Longhurst. By cunningly appearing to wish to keep players out of the competition and limiting the number of spectators on the course (one must apply for tickets next year the day after the competition closes) Mr Clifford Roberts has turned the Masters into the prestige event of all golf. Even the TV companies are limited to two commercials a session: yet they pay thousands for the honour.

The later history of Gamesmanship is more complex. Women play their part, and will be treated in their place. Golfing nations mutiply, and they intermix. Later in the book it may be possible to observe styles with the fine adjustment, to distinguish between the manly simplicity of the Canadian style, and the delicate cross-hatching of the Japanese pattern. These things will be dealt with in their place, if there is any nation which we can mention at the time of writing without being frightfully careful what we say about it.

One word of warning. There is in modern sport a remarkable tendency to bad manners, unsporting play, unfriendliness and loss of temper. It is one thing not to smile: looking cross is something else altogether. Football journalists have sometimes called roughness and rule breaking 'gamesmanship', for the simple reason that since the first gamesmanship publications, the word by constant repetition has in some quarters lost its original meaning, and acquired a coarser significance, which has nothing to do with the complex of behaviours implied in the true definition. A note of mine recently published in *The Times* will explain my point in terms of golf.

'*The Times* has hitherto been meticulously accurate in its use of the term. To see ... "gamesmanship" turned into an antonym of "sportsmanship" will give pain to many... Your correspondent in an otherwise excellent and much needed article, praises *by contrast* the "behaviour of Palmer, who once drew attention to the fact that, unobserved, he had by accident incurred a penalty of one stroke." The true gamesman would be the first to do this, though he would certainly time his action to make sure it had the maximum effect, particularly on his opponents.'

Not Gamesmanship:

(*Top*) 'Show me your card please.'

(*Bottom*) Therese Leseur was suspected, when handing in her card for the monthly medal, of not recording an air shot in a bunker.   *Blackheath: 1885.*

3
PRE-GAME PLAY

. . . start getting at your man early.

SOWING THE SEED

WHAT is the first rule of gamesmanship? To start early. Days, weeks before there is a chance of an actual contest, start getting at your man. Sow the seed of doubt.

For instance, you may like to suggest that although you have practically given up golf yourself and so are now, presumably, a 12 handicap, mid-eighties man (no need to mention that last time it was 93), yet the fact remains that when you *did* play golf you must have been pretty good because you knew people whose names appear, or perhaps used to appear, in the golf news.

Great care is necessary here. The spread of the Life-manship cult from the Western to the Eastern world has made us wincingly conscious of such coarse plays as name-dropping. Phrasing and cadence is everything. Here is a contrast:

WRONG: Bob said to me 'Look, Jim, always keep your weight on the right foot in those tricky little bunker shots if you want a spot of carry.'

RIGHT: I understand from Jones that the way to get distance from sand is to keep your weight on the right foot.

Beginners will be interested to know that a gold medallist in gamesmanship is able to suggest by his way of saying 'Jones' that Mr Bob Jones is a real friend, and that in private they Christian name each other right left and centre.*

In the same way 'coarse course-dropping' is worse than useless. 'I once played golf at Cypress Point,' says the novice, and everybody is silent, regards him as a failure and pities his frowsy phrasing. Here is the model we recommend. Its advantages are obvious:

'The 2nd at Carnoustie and the 14th at Cypress Point are almost identical. Have you noticed it?'

When choosing a course for your match, if Opponent suggests Shirley Beeches, (or whatever it is) say either (*a*) that you've never heard of it or (*b*) 'That is where I won my first little competition.' No need to name any light-hearted conditions or peculiar rules, if such there were.

ON THE DAY

On the day before the match, sound work can be done by ringing up twice. Thus:

* Or alternatively, that they were intimate enough actually to indulge in the crisp interchange of surnames.

'You're O.K. for tomorrow, of course?'

'Oh yes?'

'Excuse me ringing but you are sometimes a little *vague-o*! Anyhow I've booked a time and done all that sort of thing.'

This was the method of Walter Rimming – one of the best, as we shall see, of pre-game players. He realized such reminders had a particular irritation because one time in six he himself would forget the date completely, and be found to have left for Nottingham.

Rimming was in his lawn tennis days a specialist in what was originally called (1947) 'The Flurry'. First used for lawn tennis matches, this was essentially a plan to get your opponent to call for you by car, to keep him waiting in order to evoke an atmosphere of lateness and then to emphasize the necessity of being early. When Rimming heard your car honking outside, he would appear at the window with a newspaper in one hand and a piece of marmaladed toast in the other. Waving the toast and slowly nodding, he would start opening the door 5 minutes later, still nodding, and then remember he had not got his tennis shoes.

Curiously enough, the execution of the Flurry, designed by the gamesman to increase tension, was discovered to work in favour of the other side in the case of moving ball games, by speeding up reflexes. It was at once discarded, and only in 1958 was it realized (by Coad and Harley Chubb simultaneously) that the whole gambit was ideally suited to offensive pre-play in golf.*

Henry Cotton, on a match day, always insisted on somebody else driving him to the course in his own

* And, in a lesser degree to all still ball games, especially croquet, and bottle pool.

maroon Mercedes, if possible a rival competitor. Cotton would relax, with eyes half-closed. G. D. Scatter, of Chelmsford (15) is said to have won 3 consecutive monthly medals using this method and no other.*

Scatter avoiding tension.

Driving to the course, your conversation in the car must be carefully chosen. Something on the lines of 'Sorry I can't play on Sunday' may be of some use.

OPPONENT (*who is playing with somebody else on Sunday anyhow*): Oh can't you?

GAMESMAN: I think Sunday morning should be for the children, don't you?

If Opponent has children, however old,† he may be put slightly on defensive.

Or Gamesman may say: 'It's the day we set aside for our children's old nurse. She's 69, you know. Still marvellous.'

This can be quite effective if, as you happen to know, opponent is 69 himself.

---

* The techniques of Rimming and Scatter are described in more detail at the end of this chapter.

† I happened to know that the two children of Oldmaster, for instance (a frequent user of this ploy) were aged 42 and 45 respectively.

THE GRIP

At the club-house, it often happens that one of the opponents in your four ball is a stranger, to whom you will be introduced.

Old fashioned books on golf used to start with a chapter on 'The Grip', meaning the way to hold a golf

Opponent (right) *has just read book on grip.*

club. Golf writers seem to pride themselves on being able to go on for ages about this fuss-pot subject. One often sees victims of these writers taking hold of their club one finger at a time, as if they were learning the clarinet, or trying to avoid something sticky. Yet who

A straight-in-the-eye stare makes Opponent feel as if his handicap was suspect.

has written a single sentence on the correct method, when greeting him, of gripping or not gripping the hand of the man who is going to play against you?

Yet procedure at this point can often affect the whole game.

CLUB-HOUSE PRELIMINARIES

Club-house Play is not fully active until the round is over (see Chapter 9), but this is the place to say a word about clubs and clothes. Here the basic law which I outlined in 1947 still holds good. BE THE OPPOSITE. The best counter to a streamlined set of matched woods and matched irons is still a few oddments looking as if they had been picked up individually from a railway lost property office. What we *have* done, and we hope it will prove popular, is to make available our set now known as 'Yokel' (the Gamesmanship Unmatched). This is based on individual unmatched clubs as used by well-known unmatched players. These include, for instance:

Darwin's 'Big Bertha', a very big bladed niblick with a cutting edge which can be used as an 8, 9 or sand-iron. Old Mother Bushbury's Baffy. Modelled on a 5 wood, with its shortish shaft and heavily weighted head, this club is, we believe, likely to quench the smile on Opponent's face when he thinks 'My God, he's taking that fearful club to get him out of heather.' Our 'Stainfast' No. 3 iron has a half-erased 'mid-iron: Mac Smith' engraved on its worn back. The club is steel shafted but completely non-rust-proof.

Queer clubs and special gadgets are highly vulnerable to gamesmanship and are not recommended. The man with the gleaming matched set can rescue his status by saying 'I was asked to try these out'. As a curiosity one remembers Major Cornpetter's one club (now disallowed) which could be put at any desired degree of loft by adjusting a ratchet. He annoyed casual opponents by taking his time over this and by

screwing an eyeglass into his eye before each man-
oeuvre. It made us angry because we all knew this was
another example of Cornpetter's *golfing meanness* (see
p. 64) and determination not to spend money in the
shop.

(see p. 64)

AN OLD RULE

'Be the opposite' still holds good so far as clothes are
concerned. It is no good members of the Old Gamesman's Brigade attempting to vie with the standards of
dress followed by their club professional. T. Rattigan
was an exception, especially in wet weather, when his
mackintosh tie, and mackintosh left hand glove, and
mackintosh receptacle for mackintosh accessories are
still spoken of.

But G. Paine points out (November 1967) that there
is today something suspect about the wearing of *any
kind of mackintosh whatever*, and to do so is reminis-
cent of the golfing jacket of ill fame, still seen in the
wardrobe of non-clothesmen. This is not only because
mackintosh does not slide over mackintosh, but because it is bad style games play to refer to any form of
moisture on the golf course, particularly rain.

To the fully aware winter golfer it is going to be
either a one-, two- or three-sweater day. If rain
threatens, then Operation Powder-dry will swim
smoothly into action. A special rain-trained caddy is a
necessity rather than a luxury. He will be expert in the
handling of towels, and other xerogenic devices. Umbrella drill is faultless, and even when it is absolutely
pouring and Clothesman is thinking 'now I certainly
can't get the 14th green in three', his actual spoken
comment will be:

'This should make the 14th easier.'

The non-O.K.-ness of the golf jacket is an example of the great clothes law that No Garment Should Be Quite Sensible. The all-important golf shoe, strong yet flexible, with long prehensile nails, is rescued from the boringly logical by an elegantly wasteful use of leather in the tongue. When the licensee of the Cambridge Arms was asked by the Secretary of the North Hants Club not to play golf with the ends of his trousers tucked into his socks, he resigned. Yet what a sensible thing to do, on a muddy day. But, as Longhurst reported at the time:

Clubs divide themselves inexorably into those where you tuck your trousers into your socks and those where you don't.

We are working at the moment on ways of being more careful versus less careful, in summertime golf clothes. To what extent is it all right to wear neither a tie nor a scarf on the course and if neither what is there to prevent a Hemingway type from undoing the top two buttons of his sports shirt? And where does one go from there? On sunny days Tickler, while waiting for his opponent to go through the putting ritual, would stand face full to the sun with his eyes shut and his sports shirt practically open to the navel – behaviour which made someone like Sir Barnett Gelper straighten his tie and retire into his shell more completely than ever, especially if Tickler said:

'Nothing like ultra-violet, Gelper.'

Gelper's own complexion, so far as the state of being able to get brown was concerned, long having passed the point of no return.

Superiority of some detail of equipment may be the

basis of a minor ploy, before or during a match. Buffalo Strang would talk about shoes, in his confident way, as Wiffley the unconfident was coming out of the changing room.

'Let's look at the soles of your shoes, Wiffley.'

Wiffley of course made the mistake of actually lifting one foot, and wobbling. One couldn't help thinking of Tickler's bad joke about Wiffley being 'born prematurely'.

'You're never going to get a grip with that, are you?' Strang was booming. 'The nails must be in a 3–2 grouping. It sort of sucks you *into* the ground instead of pushing you off it.'

Wiffley would have the feeling, on the 1st tee, that he was sliding about on soap.

HOW TO PLAY THE COURSE

If gamesman is host to friend who does not know course, he must remember that his opponent is two up from the start if only because he's supposed, because of

this ignorance, to be two down. Any advice given must of course be perfectly genuine.

'Now this is our 4th and we're rather proud of it.'

Cornpetter used to say this, extending arm and raising two fingers.

'Ideally your drive should pitch two fingers to the right of a line on the railway signal. Got it?'

Though correct, this exact instruction may lead to 'warped steering' of the ball. But you should early implant an atmosphere of good fun into the game.

'As long as we have a pleasant afternoon and a *really good game* – that's the point, isn't it?' This always made Wiffley, a 16 who was really 24, feel that he was going to lose the match 8 and 7.*

ON THE FIRST TEE

Many golfers have been frightened all their lives of the first tee. This is precisely the kind of situation where, difficult as it is, gamesmanship can be of some help.

What is the predominant feeling as we wait on this tee? It is fear. How can we counteract – gain advantage? Quite often on this tee there are tall youths waiting to drive off. As they take practice swings, the earth trembles, the air sings, with the speed of their clubheads through that vast arc. You will feel inclined to take no practice swing at all because you know your swing may either make no sound whatever, or merely hit the ground a puny 'bonk' and stop there.†

* Ackminster had an excellent counter to the 'two fingers' business. Starting with 'Er' he said: 'Actually in the Gunners we used to say two *knuckles* to the right, not two fingers, for fire orders. Supposed to be a slightly more accurate estimate of ... 8 degrees, I suppose. Were you thinking in terms of 8 degrees?' This last question was so irrelevant that Cornpetter, feeling that he had been made to look out of date anyhow, drove straight into the rushes.

† Golfade Ltd. provide a tiny device easily attachable to the clubhead, 'practically invisible', and costing only 6/11. The

One is waiting on the tee before driving. A pause. A bit of a hold up. Two couples to play before you. Before being caught up in the game, one's mind is a confusion of golf and non-golf thoughts, fag ends of anxieties, attempts to remember the time you drove beyond the bunker at the 7th last Saturday and what it was you did right mixed up with an attempt to work out why Senator Kodex drifted away from you at the party, and what possessed you to make a sort of *financial boast* to Jean? Here on this haunted square of turf, when the golfer is at his most vulnerable, the gamesman should be at his most alert. Yet too often he lets the opportunity slip.

A few suggestions. If opponent starts to talk about golf, walk five paces away and stare in the opposite direction. Make him feel as if he were talking in church.

Usually, in our lot, there was silence while the half-dozen or so waited. Tickler used this fact to make tastelessly timed introductions.

'Let's see, do you know Major Cornpetter?' he would say. 'This is "Tootles" Austin,' he would go on, using a little-known nickname, which Austin hated. Later Tickler would be heard whispering that Austin was 'shy'.

The worst thing that Tickler did was to choose the wrong time to tell a funny story, and if there is a worst time, it is on the first tee.

'I've told you the story about Spears on the 1st tee at Moujins,' he would begin.

'Yes,' Cornpetter would say.

'About the little man with a limp in front?' Tickler

'Atom Rocket' (to speak the language of their advertizing) 'makes your club go SWISH-WHISTLE-WOOSH'. It is quite useless.

would go on, laughing as if the whole world was laughing with him. 'Who turned out to be Field-Marshal Lord Methuen,' said Cornpetter, in a dead voice. But Tickler simply doubled up at this reminder.

There are ways of increasing first tee tension, or reversing it. Young Cornpetter knew that his father the Major disapproved of his longish hair. He would, when playing *against* his father and waiting to play before strangers, take out a pocket comb.

In foursome play Ackminster, who was a bit of an all-rounder, used to say to his opponents: 'Let's see, which of you is first string?' This is a phrase from rackets, and it is accepted that rackets is a more esoteric game than golf. (G.P.)

But my model for first tee behaviour has always been G. Paine. He is simple, he is quiet. He stands a little apart. He takes no practice swings with driver. Calling for a number 6, he holds it in his left hand and makes a gentle stroking motion grazing the turf. Nothing more.

CONTRASTED STYLES OF RIMMING AND SCATTER

I am one who finds it easier to understand history in terms of personality; and to feel that the Corn Laws, for instance, can best be comprehended by reading the correspondence, serialized with pictures, of John Bright's first secret girl friend. Let me, then, finish this chapter with a fuller account of the contrasted techniques and golfing personalities of Rimming and Scatter.

Scatter was rather podgy, but Rimming had a hook nose with a cardboard-thin bridge, eager, hungry-looking eyes and a mouth which tended to go down at the corners. With his putter's stoop he was a typical 11 handicap, with a fanatical eye for detail. His watchword was 'relax', yet his very way of saying this seemed to wind his opponents up to bursting point. His oft reiterated axiom was 'Don't press', yet through some instinct he induced the 'press' atmosphere wherever he played.

Rimming did the organizing, Scatter did the work. On the transport side, it always seemed to be Scatter who had to drive Rimming to the course. They usually played at Woking; and, of course, Rimming kept his opponent waiting.

'We'd better press on,' he said as he came out of his house. Then:

'Let's see, what's *your* way to Woking?'

'Well, I usually go via the water-works,' said Scatter, who got a bit waisty in later years, owing to his habit of having no lunch, which meant eating ginger biscuits all the morning.

'All right, let's try it.'

'That's what we usually do.'

'I know, but let's keep going.'

At the first traffic block Rimming would purse his lips. 'We're awfully near Kempton,'* he would say.

SCATTER: But it's 9.30 – surely the first race isn't till two?

RIMMING: I know, but it's all the hangers-on and the hucksters and the outside men in their cars. The trainers and the tipsters. The coke merchants and the whelk stalls and their women – all the paraphernalia, and the splendid nonsense, the doodah and the how d'you-do. Do you remember Frith's picture?

SCATTER: O.K., O.K.

RIMMING: You might have turned left at Job's Dairy. (*Then, nearing the club-house*) There's plenty of time.

This would give the impression that they had to adhere to some kind of timetable. Rimming's guest would be vaguely surprised to find the course almost empty.

In the changing room Rimming would always be ready two minutes before anybody else. He had learned rapid changing from an old actor friend of his who, though he was recently miscast as Firs in *The Cherry Orchard*, had once been a quick-change artist successful in Glasgow Vaudeville.

'We'll just get off before Old Galloway if we're quick,' Rimming would say. At once Scatter would break a shoelace.

But Scatter gave Rimming a good match. He had his own unobtrusive style of gamesmanship. Basically it

* Celebrated South English race-course then in way of most routes from London to golf.

was a Please Look After Me approach. Scatter was incapable of mending anything or renewing something worn out. Never known to buy new windscreen wipers, he would cause delays, when driving to the golf course in a slight drizzle, by turning on wipers from which every particle of rubber had been worn. This made a squeaking sound and covered the screen with a thin semi-circle of mud. There was a stair rod in his house

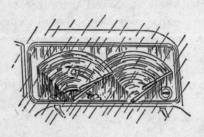

which had been loose for seven years. One after one his shoelaces would go till he had only one pair left. In the changing room he had to swap over the laces from his ordinary shoes to his golf shoes. This residual pair of laces was made of leather, difficult to insert, which doubled the impatience of Rimming and at this point Scatter's last decent lace always broke. Even I was liable to miss my first drive after this sort of thing, but I enjoyed a three ball with these two. One could be certain that there would be something wrong with Scatter's trolley. Sometimes the bottom of his golf bag came off. Rimming would sacrifice a handkerchief to tie it on. Eventually our three might very well actually be holding up a 4-ball coming up behind.

'Your putt,' Rimming would say, in a voice like a bacon-slicer. But I knew Scat's putter. The grip was continuously unwinding and had to be tied in a knot before he could play. By now we were all on edge, and when, at the next hole, it was discovered that Scat's foot kept coming out of his shoe, now laceless, the inevitable jamboree of pressing and topping started.

In the end I would say it was Scatter who had won. Beneath Rimming's 11 handicap fixation was a kind heart. Scat aroused what can only be described as a maternal instinct in Rimming. He would follow him round like a nursemaid, finally fixing the grip of his putter and quietening, with oil, the scream from the left wheel of his trolley. I don't know who won the gamesmanship but I do know that it was Scatter who knocked out Rimming in the William Bowles Trophy, Scatter who won the leather bridge marker.

4

REAL HANDICAP

THE PROBLEM STATED

BEFORE we get on to the gamesmanship of actual golf play, one other preliminary must be analysed, and the true facts, perhaps for the first time, must be presented.

In the States, one talks of a 'mid-eighties man', 'a low seventy' and so on. In Britain we use the fine adjustment. The man who on a *good* average goes round a par 72 course in 81 is given a handicap of 9 by his Club.

This of course should make everything clear and straightforward. But in fact a large proportion of players have never had an official handicap, or, having a handicap which suits their character (seeming paradox to be explained later) will stick to this, however varying their changes of form, for thirty years. For whatever reason, in a straight match, the majority of players have not got a straight reply to the question 'What is your handicap?' because they don't know the answer.*

* This, of course, is a gamesmanship situation. Boyce always became very exact at this moment. After arranging to play for two golf balls, and being hail-fellow about this, he would change his tone, look directly at his opponent and say:

'By the way, what *is* your handicap? Mine is twelve.'

'Oh, 15, now, I suppose' is a typical answer.

This would make Boyce say 'I see.'

Opponent would feel that he was under some sort of suspicion and would be likely to try to compensate, giving opponent $3\frac{1}{2}$ foot putts.

Professionals commonly play to plus two, yet every-body knows that Nicklaus is plus 7 and poor old Joe Bloke, after forty years of plus 2, is nearer minus 7.

In other words the phrase 'What is your handicap?' is ambiguous, is based on a wrong assumption of the indestructibility of number and is ripe for a more realistic appraisal.

This we have prepared.

'HEART HANDICAP'

What is the truth behind the myth? That handicap based on a score of 91 gross in the Monthly Medal on 5 February 1958 means very little outside that round of 5.ii.58, the conditions for which *will almost certainly never be repeated*. Every player knows that his true handicap varies not only from year to year, but *between the morning and afternoon of the same day*. This is partly because weather conditions affect different players differently. Much more important is the state of body and mind. Here are some 'heart' handicaps – as the slightly over-romantic Gloria Fenn calls them.

First, a typical example. An important aid to morale is the wearing of new golf shoes, comfortable, modern, efficient, built in a profusion of good leather. We call this 'a minus two equivalent' – in other words two strokes should be taken off the handicap.

Now for a list, with values:

Life Situation	Add	Subtract
Perfect Spring Weather. Girl has refused you.	6	
Perfect Spring Weather. Girl has accepted.		6

Perfect Spring Weather. Not in love.	6
1 kümmel after lunch.	1
3 kümmel after lunch.	5
5 kümmel after lunch.	3
Your junior in the Export Division has been sent to Rome for fortnight.	3
Your office secretary suddenly bent down and kissed top of your head.	4
Still absolutely no reaction to your report which has been on controller's desk for 10 days. Amounts to deliberate rudeness?	4
Won club snooker competition day before.	2
Son associates the name 'Beethoven' with some sort of popular song.	1
Boy with really terrifyingly long hair may be going for your daughter.	4

We are working now on a method of making Gamesmanship's Heart Handicaps, or 'H.H.', practical. Just before play, competitor must spend up to four minutes in a computer booth, pushing buttons as he scans a questionnaire sheet. Ackminster, our accredited mechanic, has already gone far towards adapting a fruit machine, fantastically speeded up, to this purpose. It is capable, even on a bad day, of delivering an H.H. in 3·3 seconds.

'If only it was as simple as that,' I hear the perceptive reader saying to himself. All good books of instruction contain boldly contradictory statements, especially those on golf.

(See page 56)

HANDICAP TYPES

Parallel to, and independent of, Heart Handicaps is the fact that each *established* golfer acquires in time a fixed handicap. Handicap and player have coalesced.

It is not the characters of golfers which differ so much as the *character of their handicaps*.

Some people, unused to the pioneering discoveries of lifethought, are left breathless by such statements. But let he who says 'this is false' read through this first list of suggested handicap traits.

Take 24 as a start. This handicap for a woman is generally associated with an *ambitious nerviness* and a determination, long thwarted, to become 18. But in a man it has a suggestion of roundness and warmth. The 24 man is rarely a self deceiver. The 22 man on the other hand may be nigglingly mean and, however short

a deep-voiced 18

with his woods, a very good putter. The unusual number 21 suggests an ex 24 who has recently won a toast rack. 20s are generally past their prime but are men of spirit. This they show by saying either that they have never had a day's illness in their lives or (in alternate weeks) that they are never really free from pain.

The character of 18 is split. There is a weak and colourless 18, with thin red hair perhaps, one whose skin never browns in the sun, a flaccid personality, an acid-drop sucker, never likely to get married, the sort of man who in the country looks as if he wishes he was in a town, and *vice versa*. But there is also a deep-voiced 18, a man who has recently given up football, a man of

. . . never had a day's illness in his life.

strength, who, though often off course, can, using only a spoon and number 8, slash his way round by sheer muscle.

More thin-blooded even than the 'weak' 18 is 17, with his unpleasant eyes a pale and watery blue. He finds it difficult to get opponents or is too mousey to ask for them. Old 16s are sound sensible people who may have been 7 before the war. Young ones, or more particularly young 15s, often emphasize that they are playing 'for fun' – i.e. that they are non-golfers – and don't like people who 'take the game too seriously'.* The longest-handicap man to get the care-worn look of the really hooked or nearly hooked golfer is the 14. He spends time in the professional's shop looking at clubs, testing but never actually buying them. When he is about to address the ball he will be likely, because he has just read Gadman on *The Grip*, to take hold of the shaft with his left hand first, finger by finger, as if he were learning to play the recorder. There is a little secret something about him, which one may guess to be that he believes his handicap could just possibly be down to 12 after the next Committee Meeting. Any experienced gamesman can use this fact in the games-play.

Thirteens are rare: but 12s are all too common. This is the pleasant backwater of golf. All on a golden afternoon. Abandon ambition all ye who enter here. Twelves often chat during play. Nearly 15 per cent of the bar receipts come from 12s: and 12 is the average handicap of the Sunday four-ball quartet who have played together since 1946 or even '36. It is a rule that except for young players on the way down, 12s must never have their handicap altered until they reach the age of 85. They are not only difficult to beat in actual play; their gamesmanship is sometimes impregnable, though often primitive, (a common gambit, among old friends who play together regularly, is never to comment or change expression, even after a shot which is exceptionally good or particularly bad. Not in any situation do they say 'bad luck').

The biggest change comes with 11. At once this suggests a much more serious golfer, the highest handicap

* In fact, people who are 'against taking the game too seriously' are really taking-the-game-seriously too seriously.

player to possess an inner fire. Cheeks pale and drawn, eyes intense and often too close together, 11 will keep to his handicap but only by constant effort and practice so unremitting that it may involve some slight

... *typical 11*

physical deformity. Some 11s believe themselves to be under a curse. They seldom win the annual club knock-out.

The handicap of 10 is in strong contrast. It suggests a man more relaxed, approaching the dignity of being Good at Games. Often he belongs to the 'really better than that' brigade, e.g. 10 may be really 8. A 9, on the other hand, is often a more genuine 11, under a special strain of trying to keep to single figures. In contrast again 8 and 7, often really 5, or at any rate on their way to better play, are distinguishable because 8 is not un-happy to remain 8 as he is beginning to enjoy collect-ing twinkling silver spoons and tinkling ash trays. Difficult to deal with in play, he is vulnerable in opposition to a superior trophyman. Eight is ambi-tious, exercises his grip fingers during working hours by suddenly clutching his umbrella and practises the beginning of the swing with the right arm only, even if he is in Oporto, waiting for a taxi.

The 5 man, once he has achieved this splendidly low figure, is liable, unless he rapidly improves still further,

to become fixed in the trap of his own virtuosity. Age stops the way to advance, pride stops re-adjustment during the eternal return to double figures. He continues to come to the Club but spends his playing time on the practice ground. How well I remember W.D.J.S. of Aldeburgh, who was often seen on the putting course, bent like a croquet hoop, or far away on the practice ground, east of the 14th. In the distance the sea darkened as the sun dropped low: but W.D. would be there, putting down yet another row of 40 golf balls, to hit them distances which were gradually to decrease, if only by a foot a year, with his No. 4 iron. Five, the highest handicap to suggest 'expert', he had attained. Five he was determined to be for ever. So he remains, one of the loneliest figures in the world of games, a ghost of the practice ground or wistfully following, at a distance, the gay careless pursuers of the monthly medal or the four-ball friendly.

The 4s and under belong to a special patrician class who *could* 'go round in level fours'. They are different, they are not us; though I myself have twice done level

4s: the first time was in 1936 at Chislehurst. This subjected me ever since to the heavy-handed gamesmanship play of 'that short course at Chislehurst', until years later I was level 4s at the really tough North Berwick.*

Three always sounds, by the mere precision of the number, as if it was really 3. The brilliant figure of 2 is again associated with the anti-parallelism of the absolute opposite. Two is either a dashing all-rounder occasionally playing cricket for Kent, or a dedicated monk-like character, who lives, like one of the *pujurats* of Istambul, in a stone cell, somewhere on the outskirts of the course. Scratch has to adopt the character of the schoolboy hero, not always easy, once the mid-thirties are passed, and plus 2 belongs to yet another world, the man from H.Q., umpiring matches in the Piccadilly Tournament, a man who must never be interrupted or spoken to on duty and even off it.†

* By a ploy which came to me on the spur of the moment. After breakfast at the Hotel I strolled onto the course with my clubs, took my driver on the first tee I came to (the 14th?), topped the drive, topped my iron, took an 8 to the edge of the green and holed my putt. For once I did the right thing. I walked in. 'I didn't finish the round,' I said – and remember that this exact wording is essential – 'but when I came in I was level fours.'

† That the handicap itself suggests a character will be immediately clear if we think of figures of the pre-golf era. Everybody must agree that Julius Caesar was 11 down to the last detail of his *De Bello*, just as it is almost as clear that Pompey was a genuine 8 while Mark Antony, calling himself 6, was in fact much nearer to 16. Later on Mozart, passionately wanting to get down to single figures, was the bravest of 13s; Shakespeare would have played off the same handicap, but was too casual and absentminded. Rubens would have given even more of the painting of his paintings to staff if he had indulged his obvious talents as a long handicap liable on occasion to do 80: Hazlitt's 3 would

A FEW EXAMPLES

THE OLD QUOTESMAN

Now to examine a few handicap types in action. Let us begin with a not very typical example – a 12 playing against a 12. Some of the prettiest backwaters of gamesmanship are revealed when two men of the same kind of handicap leanings are opposed. Saxe and 'Buffalo' Strang were both of the relaxed, literary, well-read school. Both could quote.

'The play's the thing,' Strang would say as they started, and to Saxe's slight annoyance this was thought remarkable in Strang simply because he had lived for weeks in such wild sounding places as Buffalo in up state New York. As soon as Strang found himself in a bunker, 'Come unto these yellow sands,' Saxe would say. His curly white hair was suitable to this gambit, and he used a wonderfully light 'bright' voice, but he was not invulnerable. Buffalo often knew the quotation and would continue it to the end of the poem speaking with expression and keeping Saxe waiting for his shot. Even more effectively he would wait for Saxe's next bad shot, which would on average be his next but one, and say something like 'keep down, thou reverent head' in a *quoting tone of voice*. It was good to hear these two together.

---

have been coldly passionate. Everybody would have been frightened of Dido, unpopular President of Sunningdale Women : but she would have been impossible to dislodge. Shelley and Baudelaire, Swinburne and Aubrey Beardsley, would be typical non-players. Although each in their different ways were lifemen, golf gamesmen were they never.

'CORN' *versus* HARLEY CHUBB

But no doubt the purest games pleasure comes from the clash of mighty opposites. Take Major Cornpetter and Harley Chubb. If anybody says to me 'look after the pennies' I always think *Cornpetter*. Cornpetter was a by no means effortless 8: and his tenseness expressed itself in an unreasonable desire to save money. At home he would produce quite decent champagne at a cocktail party, but as soon as he got near a golf course he would begin saying things like 'the price of sandwiches nowadays!'

'Gone up?' said Chubb, a relaxed 15.

'Everything. Do you know when I first started playing a caddy got 2/6d a round, tip included?'

'I knew it was a long time ago.' Cornpetter carried his clubs himself, cramming them into a bag which compared with the pantechnicons then fashionable, looked scarcely bigger than a finger-stall.

'And paint –'

'What paint?'

'Well, the paint for repainting repaints.'

This sort of thing took the carnival out of golf as effectively as anything I know, but not for Cornpetter. He would make a great point of coming out with only two peg tees. He actually boasted of this with a sort of frosty twinkle. In June when the grass was long, the only person who helped Cornpetter look for his tee was one new member. But Corn always came back with more tees than he started out with. When plastic bags were introduced he tied his tee to one of them with string. It was rather useful in a ghastly way, acting as a parachute.

Cornpetter only became really frightening, however,

when he went off with somebody to play on a course to which neither of them belonged. Once Corn and I had to attend a dinner in Birmingham. 'Let's play Little Aston tomorrow,' he said. We were staying in the same hotel. He insisted on breakfast at 7.30 sharp.

'May as well get our moneysworth out of the course,' he said, knowing that I made it a rule not to get up early in the Midlands.

'Unless of course we start after 4 o'clock: then we get in half price.'

'For God's sake,' I said, but I was feeling floppy.

'We could go and look at the Pre-Raphaelite collection. It's worth seeing.'

This annoyed me too (a) because Corn had certainly never seen the Birmingham Gallery and (b) because I had just been reviewing a book called *Fidella: Mother of Holman Hunt*. Something made me uneasy. I said:

'You've got some sort of introduction to Little Aston, I suppose?'

'I've got my Automobile Association card. But they're longing for people like us.'

I'd heard Corn say this before. The essential thing was to pay before we played. I steered him to the bar to get signed in. At once he ordered a drink.

'No hurry,' he said. 'It might start to rain. Or we might see someone we know. Save us a dollar.'

I've known Corn say to a complete stranger in the changing-room: 'Pardon me, sir, but do you know if it's possible for strangers to play here?'

Often he gets the reply: 'It's quite simple, you just pay thirty bob.' But nothing stops him. He will say to the steward:

'I'm supposed to be "doing" these golf courses for the

B.B.C. N.B.C. are interested too. So are C.B.C....
Very.' Then his general line continues:

'Yes, sir, this is something I've longed to play all my
life. Your course. That's your famous last hole, isn't it?

'May one play here as a stranger?'

And which is your dog-leg? The 14th? It may surprise
you to know that your 14th is the most famous dog-leg
in Europe. What did Hagen say of it? ...'

If the bar was empty, Corn would secretly look at the
names, lettered in gold, of recent winners of the Captain's prize.

'Let's see ... Colonel A. J. Crombie is a member here,
isn't he?'

'Not here today, sir.'

'No – no? He always wanted "to show me himself",
he said.'

Supposing this man turned up? Upright, fair-haired,
military bearing, no doubt. All this meant that I was
going to play in a state of tension.

Once, at the height of the slump in the mid-thirties,
we had to include Corn in a 4-ball at the Bushey
course. Unemployment was high and it was all too easy
to get caddies, a big group hopefully waiting near the

first tee, a ragged regiment. Everyone was determined to get one. Except Corn.

'Your honour,' we said. He drove rather low and hit the ladies tee-box 20 yards ahead so hard that the ball bounced back over our tee, over our heads and *over the group of waiting caddies* into the wood 40 yards behind. A long, low, relaxed savouring laugh spread through us all: but it had no effect on Corn, who, believe it or not, insisted on looking for his ball for the full five minutes, methodically combing the brambles. When he emerged he held aloft three balls in his bleeding hands.

'Not bad,' he said.

The antithesis of Take-Care of the Pennies is Be-Prodigal-with-the-Pounds. Among golf gamesmen this takes a sophisticated form. One only discovers that the Poundsman is wealthy after he has been around a month or two. Even then it must *leak* out, only.

'Who's the last person in the world you would suspect of being a millionaire?'

Harley Chubb didn't mind it at all when Cuffey said this.

Harley certainly had the cash all right and he made good use of it. He had a Continental Bentley, of course, but the car he picked you up in, (battling against the wind on the way to his Eastbourne Downs Course) was a 1933 Hispano with headlights like soup tureens, a car so Sports that it seemed, and felt to the passenger, even more open with the hood up. One arrived deeply cold, in a meaningless way.

Harley was never a coarse pound player: but even the back of his pink and prosperous neck seemed to proclaim that he was playing for very much lower stakes than his normal. If he won ten shillings, he would change it into sixpennies in the bar and then pour it down the fruit machine under the hungry eyes of Cuffey, whose father paid for him to be allowed to work.*

* 'T' – I won't give his name – used to carry round £4 worth of sixpennies in a cotton bag. 'I'll just put one in for luck' he'd say just before we started for the first tee. We would hear the familiar clicks and then – the sound of a shower of sixpences. 'Jack-pot' sang T and was seen quietly picking up his 'win'. 'Why him?' thought little Cuffey, as intended, and topped his first iron shot 20 yards along the ground.

5
PRIMARY PLAY

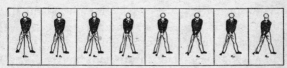

1–2. Why didn't the steward say 'Good morning'? 3 Getting above himself. 4 Well, it's his loss. I'm not going to press him. 5 Must ring Cornelia. 6–7 Do I really want to go to the Magic Flute or is it just her? 8 'Be conscious of the right hand' he said.

THE SWING

'Look out,' he said, just as Big Jim Dougan was about to drive. 'There's a fly on the ball. Stand back and start all over again.'

This ploy from an early gamesmanship school story may seem naïve yet it demonstrates well the truism that the first object of the gamesplay should be to break flow, and the second to introduce non-golf thoughts in the swing and the golfgame.

How many people realize that every part of the swing is associated with irrelevant and putting-off thoughts? It is these irrelevant thoughts, always latent, which the gamesman must try to bring to the surface, however buried and fleeting they may be.

PLAYING FOR MONEY

'What shall we play for?'
'You say.'

The man who says 'you say' is one up. It suggests that to play for half-a-crown would be amusing but that his ancestors, members of White's Club to a man, were equally prepared to stake an estate or a mistress on a game of shove-groat or 'Rock-i'-the-Ring'. Opponent is likely to suggest playing for something decidedly larger than is usual for him. May I tentatively suggest for this occasion a new ploy I am provisionally calling 'To-him-that-hath-shall-be-givenmanship' may be tried? Let slip suggestions that there is wealth in your family. Say 'Have you got a car coming for you?' (suggesting chauffeur *milieu*) or 'Father has been asked to lend his Bernardino Taddi for next year's Quattrocento Italian exhibition at the R.A.' (picture worth £100,000). This will bring in the unbreakable rule of money play:

> If stake is more than mother says
> Ah then 'tis you it is who pays.'*

BASIC

THE DRIVE

Of all the problems which face the golf gamesman, the problem of pure good play is the most difficult to fight. In particular, some of the best gamesmanship brains in America, many of them drained from England which drained them from Scotland, have been bent to the problem of how to be one-up on the man who hits the longer ball.

In normal circumstances it may be possible, for instance, to give advice to a man who is 2 or 3 up: but it is difficult indeed if he is outdriving you. A list of attempted ploys looks little better than a confession of

* The rhyming of 'says' and 'pays' shows that both were pronounced alike in 1697, when White's was founded.

failure. There is the driver from the head of which you unbutton a head cover marked with a large 'No. 4'. There is the remark, if your own drive of 150 yards happens just to have cleared the rough on the right, that 'position is the point here, not distance'.*

Then there is the old ploy, first mentioned by me in 1947, of giving your Vast Distances man a caddy who never says 'good shot' but often points to a place, 30 yards ahead, which was reached by Byron Nelson when he played the course in 1946, or, better still, by J. H. Taylor, when he played there with a gutty in '98.

The problem will be solved in time. Funds for our Long Ball Research Wing are welcome and needed. Meanwhile let me give one piece of general advice. Never, never comment on the fact that your opponent has got distance. Never say 'You certainly powdered that one'.† Puzzled by your silence, long driver will try to outdistance even himself until, inevitably, he ends up out of bounds.

But the important point to remember is that superiority in length is a myth, or is at any rate cancelled out by relativity. It depends on the standard of measurement. The man who is outdriven at Sandwich can always say 'when Sarazen won here he never used

---

* My wife heard a celebrated version of this ploy when we were watching the pro-amateur at Seminole, Fla. There was a new young professional, Mike Souchak, under whose huge frame and footballer's feet the earth trembled. 1952 was a successful year for him on the circuit 'because he had learned to reduce the length of his drive'. We passed this on to Wiffley, J., (16) of our Club.

† It is still more important to warn your female partner, in a foursome, especially if she is your wife, not to say 'Ooo' or give a little scream of female admiration. Tell her to say 'Well, he got away with that one.'

more than a 3 wood'. A following breeze may help you to make the 200 yard mark down wind at the 18th at St Andrew's. But if your opponent beats you by his usual fifteen yards it is usually safe to say:

'Amazing to think that in these conditions Nicklaus *reached the green* in all four rounds of the open.'

Wrong attitude of female partner
to male opponent.

Safe unless you are up against a St Andrew's type gamesman who will probably say:

'Yes. I wonder what club he used from the tee. After all, two generations ago Blackwell reached the *steps leading up to the club-house* with a gutty.'

It might be added here that the inferior player should never, never in any way behave differently, let alone apologize, because he is inferior. In the days when I was genuinely young and had muscles like whipcord I used to drive nearly 210 yards on the downhill hole at Redhill. My father's best was 140 yards. As soon as he had struck one of these hundred-and-forty-yarders, he would stand stock still gazing after the ball till it had stopped and then pace the distance, counting out loud, and ending in a crescendo 'a hundred and thirty-eight, *thirty-nine*, FORTY'.

It is worth noting here that if Long Handicap is playing Short – 14 playing 4, for instance – never must 14, if he wins, admit, recall, apologize or refer in any way to the fact that he has received 8 strokes in the round; and it is most unusual to refer to this when telling the story to family, particularly wife.* This situation and its handling shows yet once again the deep relationship between life and golf, of which life is so often the metaphor or mime.

STYLE

This is the place to say something not about the style of gamesmanship but the gamesmanship of style. A perfect, flowing, model style can be alarming to an opponent. The teaching of golf is not our domain: but the teaching of style comes very much into our orbit. An appearance of a strong effortless style, flowing yet built on a stable foundation, can be alarming to an opponent even if it has no effect on one's shots.

'Right, let's have a game then,' says Jeremy Cardew to comparative stranger after a dinner party.

'I haven't played for ages,' he goes on. Though in

* Tickler, having won the Doverbridge Tea-tray playing off 16, used to like putting on the special Tea-tray tie, particularly when he was playing against men whom he had just beaten in this competition, men who had given him perhaps as much as nine strokes.

full evening dress, he may pluck a bamboo stick from a pot in the conservatory and begin to take a practice swing, left hand only.

'My, what a wide arc to that swing,' thinks Wiffley, who is already wondering if he, too, ought to have worn a white tie instead of a black. We recommend the suggestion of great width, on this back-swing, and long relaxed follow-through.

Above all we recommend practising a practise swing which ends with the body turned correctly square to

Note that actual style of right-hand *figure is fractionally better.*

the direction of the ball, the hands held high, an expression of easy confidence on the face, a touch of nobility, as if one were looking towards the setting sun. Students who find themselves unable even vaguely to simulate a graceful finish may do well by going to the opposite extreme. It is possible to let go of the club almost completely at the top of the swing, recover it, and by a sort of half-paralysed jerk come down again more or less normally. Opponent will find himself *forced to stare at you,* and may lose his rhythm.

STRAIGHT LEFT ARM: A PERSONAL CONFESSION

I am sometimes asked which, of all the gambits I have invented, do I personally find most useful. Here, exclusively and for the first time, let me reveal the answer to this question.

In *Lifemanship* it is either 'Yes, but not in the South' (when Man who has Actually Been There is holding forth as if he alone, therefore, had any right to speak about the subject). Or perhaps it is the use, in motoring, of 'Plaste's Placid Salutation' (recorded in *One-Upmanship*).

In golf I have no doubt. Described in *Gamesmanship*, it is for use against the man who is driving farther and less erratically than yourself.

'I see how you're doing it,' you say, 'straight left arm at the moment of impact, isn't it? Do you mind if I stand just *here* and watch?'

In spite of the fact that the left arm is always straight at the moment of impact, this used to cause a pull in the old days. Now there is a well-developed counter.* But in '68 I am still finding it useful.

LATER HISTORY OF THE FRITH-MORTEROY

Long before gamesmanship was invented, competitors in any sport used to use game leg play – 'my leg is troubling me a little today'. Gamesmanship described its use in lawn tennis and produced the famous Frith-

---

* Driver says 'do you mean like this?' and if drive is unsatisfactory takes out another ball and drives again as if first drive was for demonstration only. 'Now let's watch *your* arm,' he then says.

Morteroy counter – the pause, half-way through the second set, the grave smile, the reference to the 'ticker' and the 'I'm supposed not to hit the ball too hard'.

All this was almost immediately taken up by golfers, as we hoped it would be. Equally predictable was it that ripostes suitable for golf were found to the Morteroy counter. Indeed a splendid gamesfield was at once exposed and I was lucky enough to be within earshot of one match played between experts in this technique.

The venue was in the Isle of Mull, with its delicate colouring, dignified coast line and views of Gaelic place names, superb fishing and a distant sight of nervy looking stags, for we always played golf in the stalking season.

The golf-course, at Tobermory, is 9 hole; it is typically Highland – i.e. equal in effort to the playing of 27 holes in Leeds Castle Park. Two or three holes involve driving across a vast valley or *druchaid*. In this foray I saw it was Seligmann against Saxe. So far as golf was concerned, Seligmann was better than Saxe, as one would expect from their handicaps, Seligmann being a clicketty-click 14 and Saxe a soft-centred 12.

Climbing up to the second tee to play up to the Hole o'Crest, Seligmann began to use his club as a stick. By the time he had reached the green he was limping. Saxe might at this point say:

'O.K.?'

'Yes – yes, perfect,' Seligmann replied: though a hundred yards farther on he would give a curious sideways kick with his left leg.

'They tell me I've got to have this op,' Seligmann remarked to Saxe, who was taking no notice.

Thus was the scene set for the counter to Game Leg

Play; and sure enough, at the top of the second hill Saxe said classically:

'Sorry, I've got to stand still for two seconds. Nothing to worry about.'

Seligmann kept his head.

'Yes, well,' he went on at once, 'as I was saying, the end of the hip bone fits into the socket or acetabulum. While we're waiting I'll draw it for you . . .'

At first Seligmann did well simply by taking no notice of Saxe's troubles – did well that is until yet another deer-stalking man joined our little party at Knock. This was Boyce, a red-hot 10, and it was he who, in our 4-ball, all against all, out Seligmanned

'Sorry, I've got to stand still for two seconds.'

Seligmann. Boyce had never held down a job for more than a year but Boyce had this remarkable pet subject, knowledge of medical terms. His study was full of pale blue piles of the *British Medical Journal*. He had Gray's *Anatomy* and the nineteenth-century edition of Stedman's *Medical Dictionary* which Tickler and Odoreida – both of them, rather surprisingly, part of Seligmann's circle – liked to look at because it was illustrated, rather thrilling if one was a layman, which speaking personally one wasn't.

I first noticed Boyce for his deft treatment of our (5) man Cardew, a bit of a hero at Old Soaking, who was having lessons from Campion, then the pro at Royal Hampton. 'How's it going?' Boyce asked him.

'Marvellous. Campion really gave me an *image*; for a bit I knew what hitting was all about.'

'Oo – I bet you did.'

'How do you mean?'

'I only mean that Campion plays every day and he's a man of *immense strength*. He can break your back, you know. That full professional swing puts a huge strain on the deep muscles of the back, especially the *transverso-spinalis* system with the – what's it called – *semispinalis capitis*?'

At Tobermory I remember that at the 4th, second time round, Seligmann, finding himself 3 down, was glad to get one back by holing a long putt.

'I say,' he said, 'somebody pick that ball out for me. Suddenly I can't stoop.'

He only vaguely knew Boyce, who was on to the situation like a knife. However Boyce said nothing.

On the next tee Seligmann reiterated his point by slowly sinking on to both knees to fix his peg into the hard ground.

'Afraid I shan't be getting any distance,' he said.

'You were always pretty short,' said Boyce.

'I can't turn my hip,' said Seligmann, smiling as if not complaining though in pain. He had never pivoted in his life. 'Maybe a slipped disc.'

'So *that's* turned up again, has it?' Boyce said. 'Probably it's just O.A.'

Seligmann didn't get it.

'Forgive me; it's just a technical term for Old Age. Anybody over the age of 45 suffers a slight disintegration of the bone structure and the joint mechanism. Splendid view.'

Round the corner below there was a huge chunk of sea, which was just beginning to roughen up.

'The wrinkled sea beneath him crawls,' said Saxe, always a bit of a quotesman.

'And there's a slight diminution of the intervertebral spaces,' Boyce continued as they walked to their respective drives. 'Staggering, isn't it?' he went on, gazing out to sea. 'In the distance you can see McCoutinglass's Mouse-trap.'

'Criminy,' said Seligmann with his smile, but he was being out-gambited and he knew it. Boyce was well ahead, on the other side of the fairway.

'Your spine begins to SHUT UP LIKE A TELE-SCOPE,' Boyce called out in a high, cheerful, carrying voice, rather throaty. 'They call it the CONCER-TINA EFFECT.' Seligmann looked round to see if anyone was listening. Boyce was pointing to an un-interesting rock which he said was called Coolie Mc-Coulin's Collar-stud.

'No, actually,' Boyce went on quietly when they had to wait on the next tee. 'You're rather a marvel. Let me look at your spine. Very little kyphosis. Think of Lionel – on two sticks now.'

'Hooray,' said Seligmann: but he never played with Boyce again.

Boyce certainly did well with his medical know-ledge. Three or four members of his Club – we all know who – began to suffer from hypochondria. It was said that Wiggs, now, never touched spirits before 10.30 a.m.

'Have you noticed?' Boyce would begin. 'Strang is developing quite a tremor of the right hand.'

'How do you mean?'

'I simply just mean it trembles slightly. Watch it

when he's bending down to put his ball on the peg, first thing.'

Boyce went through six members of the Club in the same way. 'Look at that walk,' he would say. In the end he was bound to describe some hitherto unsuspected weakness of his opponent, or better still, create an imaginary one.

In the twenties the average age at Mid Surrey was high, and they knew it. There was said to be a Death Expectancy Chart above the Secretary's desk. I do know that in the doorway, only half hidden, was a hand ambulance in wickerwork for collecting coronaries in the summer months.

As our techniques get nearer to the ultimate margins of human character, as the psychologies merge with the psychoses, we may have to pass forwards towards, or perhaps we should say fall backwards on, one of the most questionable questions in Gamesmanship.

It is this: 'Do you yip?'

Readers are reminded that the word 'yip' was invented by T. D. Armour the great teacher of golf and a fine teacherman as well. I once watched him working his way through what I hope and believe was a very profitable morning's instruction near Palm Beach. Comfortably seated in a shady arbour, with a large glass at his elbow, he sat relaxed while pupil after pupil twisted and turned in the heat of the Florida sun.

Armour defines 'yips' as a 'brain spasm which impairs the short game'. 'Impairs' is a euphemism. Since Hogan has stepped down from the throne, thousands of spectators have suffered with him as he stands motionless over his putter unable to move it. The disease seems to affect men of highly strung and subtle temper who have practised an art too long or with too dedicated a concentration. There is our own Peter Allis, with his putts; Dave Thomas with his short chips. Control of that complex joint, the elbow, seems to be lost. A great snooker player has been a victim, and a famous violinist.

No need to point out to the gamesman the uses to which these facts may be put, nor which of them to choose. No need – and on my part small desire. This is for a last resort only. There is even a possibility that during play any mention of yips, however indirect, may be banned at the next meeting of w.o.g.g.*

* The necessity of some such law was made clear when H. Longhurst reported the case of the gamesman (if indeed the man deserves such a title) who revealed before a match that he did not suffer from yips himself but 'was a carrier'.

6

SECONDARY HAMPERS

Odoreida practising the Dear Old Joe squeeze in the hamper gallery. (By permission of L.C.C. Museum, Yeovil.)

A NEW TERM NOT IN GENERAL USE

I HAVE always been surprised that my phrase 'secondary hamper' has not yet passed into current speech, although there has been comment.

Once somebody said to me, 'What does it mean, if anything?' According to the Large Oxford, the use of hamper as a noun ('something which hampers') went out of use extraordinarily suddenly, almost with a bang, in 1624, except among sea-going people. Somebody, probably a non-gamesman and trainee Roundhead, must have said, using the idiom of 1624, 'I simply can't stand that use of the word any longer.'

Interested people may like to know that I belong to a minority group – I am an anti-Jacobean Cavalier. This meant one thing only so far as 'hamper' as a noun is concerned. I had to put it back.

The meaning given to 'secondary' depends on my mood. It may be electrical – 'pertaining to an induced current'. It may be metaphorically meteorological. So much of our work is concerned with 'a subsidiary depression taking place on the border of a primary cyclone'.

GATTLING: Can't you give us a phrase for it?
SELF: Well – 'at one remove' perhaps?
GATTLING: Remove what?

Here is a simple example of the Secondary. The schoolboys are supposed to bathe in the lake on Thursdays, but it is early June, the latitude 51·09 North and the water is deadly cold. The non-gamesman boy says:

LAYBOY: Oh sir, need I bathe? I've got a splinter in my toe.

Obviously this will not work. A week later, gamesmanship-trained boy said:

GAMESBOY: Oh sir, sir, sir, you said we could bathe today, sir, sir, sir.

The master, watching the old-soldier finger snapping routine, will feel, though kindly to children, that this surely is the moment to say 'No'.*

FALSE SECONDARIES

I am 4 down to Boyce at Mid-Surrey, and I have taken the trouble to study the history of the Club. Connections with Sir Joseph Banks and Hooker, creator of Kew. Associations with George III, whose fav-

---

* Ploy suggested by L. S. L. Potter.

ourite seat was by the first bunker in front of the twelfth tee.

'That's the one,' I say, pointing to the ancient cedar.

BOYCE: What one?

SELF: The tree. The tree behind which Fanny Burney hid when George III was chasing her. He was mad, of course – off and on.

This minor distraction can be useful, especially if there is a faint trace of eccentricity in Opponent's family. Actually in this case Boyce made use of his know-all medical training.

BOYCE: As you know it's not regarded now as madness. More probably he was suffering from porphyria.

Boyce's successful parry was typical of our conversations, which were basically distraction attempts, not truly Secondary.

With the Secondary, the greater the apparent irrelevance, the bigger the effect. I was pleased to overhear this conversation, for instance, between Boyce and Cuffey, his opponent in our foursome. I think Boyce must have heard that Cuffey had come into a legacy of twenty-five pounds. Cuffey had been letting it slip right and left, as if to ask our advice. I had never seen Cuffey play a crisper game. Then, suddenly, Boyce the know-all was talking.

BOYCE: Of course there's this new thing, Amalgamated Ultrasonics.

CUFFEY: Oh yes?

BOYCE: Could put a little into that. Sorry, mustn't talk shop.

CUFFEY: Oh, I don't mind. You mean – stocks and shares?

Cuffey had never talked shop before.

BOYCE: A small group of us are buying. There is some chance that 'J.T.' may be taking over.

CUFFEY: Do you mean ...?

BOYCE (*very quiet, but very clear*): If you bought something today you would be unlikely to lose, I suppose one might say.

CUFFEY: I *seē*. Thanks most awfully.

Naturally, Cuffey's game began to collapse. He was too excited and pleased to think of golf. And at the same time he hadn't the faintest idea *what* to do, even less how to do it, and as we got near the club-house it began to prey on him.

Even experts can be momentarily shaken by this ploy. Getting away from everybody in one of my 'what's become of Potter since he gave us all the slip?' moods, I found myself in a foreign club-house, West of Marbella, on the then only half-finished golf-course of

Sotto Grande. The effect of lostness, of isolation, was spoilt by the fact that the only other person in sight turned out to be Gelper, whom I see every afternoon of my life sleeping off his lunch at the Brook Street Club. Gelper is ever involved in long term business transactions, including real estate, so when we reached the middle holes – hills have always worried Gelper – I said suddenly:

POTTER: Your people have rather missed the bus here, haven't they?

GELPER (*wheezing*): What bus?

POTTER: The value of land here is tripling, you know.

GELPER: Tripling?

Maybe I used the wrong technical term, but while Gelper was still in daze, I added something *true but irrelevant*.

POTTER: Did you know that the sand in these bunkers isn't sand? It is marble chippings.

Secondaries are by no means used to put your opponent off. Much research has gone into the perfection of phrases which will *induce your opponent to give you a three foot putt*. Nothing is published yet, but it soon became clear that although older men are less likely to grant these putts, young men induce such gestures if they choose one of the following 'conversationalized softeners' for inducing paternal protective effect:

(*a*) Play for a dollar but let it leak out that they are really desperately hard up, or would be if they weren't working their way through college by peeling potatoes in August on a Swedish timber freighter, Or (*b*) Ask questions on the technique of putting, suggesting that they regard Opponent as putting star. This should get the come-back:

'I'll give it to you, but knock it in. Remember – wrists locked.' Or

(*c*) Be so ignorant and inexperienced in worldly things that they don't know the difference between a Corporation and a Board.

But most Secondaries are involved with the kind of faint uneasiness found round the home dining table with all the children present including the older girls. Comment on the family is often directly involved. This area of play requires delicacy, for the gamesman never resorts to hurting feelings unless he is playing for really high stakes.

'I caught a glimpse of your danghter on TV yesterday,' say.

'On TV?' (*pleased*).

'Yes – in the paddock at Ascot.'

'Oh yes – yes – of course.'

'I noticed that she was smoking. Is that O.K. there now, then?'

Nothing violent here. Perfectly delicate. One could contrast this with Odoreida's oafish remark to Major Cornpetter as they walk to the 16th tee:

'I saw your boy in Curzon Street yesterday, Major. Looks as if he could do with a bit of a haircut!'

ON WITH THE MOTLEYSHIP

Reluctantly, I make a new phrase to describe what is perfectly normal and straightforward Secondary which yet has no name in our language. This gambit is rooted in the sympathy of man for man, and, again, it must not be misused, while at the same time one is bound to have to say that it is a sad comment on the world of today that it seldom comes off.

Basically this gambit consists of seeming to have a secret. The secret can be of any one of a dozen different kinds. Usually it should appear to be a sad one,* most frequently some love affair going wrong. Rough estimates suggest that letting it be known you are tremendously in love is worth a stroke if age is between 22

---

* Good work has been done recently by Cardew, who sometimes comes onto the tee and reveals a deepening appearance of having a *happy* secret, which seemingly he is not allowed to reveal, yet he appears to find it impossible to conceal an inward smile of satisfaction which remains unaffected even if he misses a short putt – death of a respected aunt, it is suggested, leaving him a pleasant legacy, or the fact that his unrespected senior in the firm never got the wall-to-wall carpet he requested for his office.

and 28, 2 strokes if under 22 and 4 strokes to the other side if over 44. Once the bloom of middle age has worn off, the adverse stroke balance may be as high as 7. If, however, you can successfully suggest to your opponent that it is he, not you, who is the subject of your girl's deepest affections, that should be, to you, no less than a 9 stroke advantage (recorded 1947).

A fruitful subject of conversation can be something connected with religion. We will deal later with the question of going to church on Sunday mornings, getting into the bar of the golf-club in nine minutes dead after the service is over and wearing your *church suit*. I am referring now to the possibility of, say, bringing up the subject of a successful and effective preacher. The brief conversation or 'parlette' can take many forms:

OPPONENT: There's obviously something good about him. [Billy Graham perhaps.]
GOLF GAMESMAN: No doubt.
O.: He rather moved me.

G.G. *should give* O. *glance and say nothing more about it whatsoever.*
Changing sides, the conversation can go like this:

O.: I see Billy Graham's here.
G.G.: Yes – next Tuesday.
O.: That turn he puts on certainly seems to get them. I suppose rather simple people...
G.G.: Yes. I'm not sure I'm not rather a simple person myself.

G.G. then gives O. a frank and open smile, which should cause O. to half-hit his pitch shot.

THE POUR

Let me end this chapter with a brief sketch of the Secondary in action. I shall not be deterred from this if it includes an incident in which I was outplayed. Boring stories about oneself in the guise of acknowledgement of a fault or admission of a defeat are part of the gamesman's armoury.

If G.G. – the Golf Gamesman – finds there is a solid two up situation developing against him, he may like to attempt The Pour, which may be defined as the emanation of a gradually developing suggestion that he is sorry but he must reveal something about his private life or burst. This can be distracting in an obvious but deep way. At first he does not reveal that he has this secret trouble except that he exhibits a temperate appearance, a tendency to silence, an intent turn of the head to his friend if he makes a remark and a quiet clear answer. Opponent may rather take a liking to this treatment.

Like many such gambits, it should only be brought into full use in the last 9 holes, and then only if still two down. At the tenth become taciturn. Then get the score wrong in favour of opponent, who may soon become suspicious. Play lightly on his nerves by assuming a kind of hesitant silence, as if wondering whether to speak. Already you may find you have got a hole back. He smells a rat. Then, quietly start pouring. 'Do you mind if I ask your advice?' you may start, or after pulling a drive, you can say in reply to

O.: Bad luck.
G.G.: I'm glad I did that.
O.: How do you mean?

G.G.: Well, if you see somebody's face on every tee box, you begin to go a little bit mad.

If one said this to Tickler he would say 'What, do you mean like the sailor on a packet of Players, sort of thing?' But the large majority of ordinary decent people will get an inkling and be prepared for your next remark.

'She wrote to me to say that she still liked me – liked me!'

This should make Opponent lose another hole, but he may lull himself with the belief that you have lost interest in the match and are playing like an automaton. This is the time to attack. Keep your head down and swing.

There is one great danger about heart-on-the-sleeve play. *It is vulnerable to the instinctive counter of the unconscious gamesman.* I tried this gambit myself once, against W. Darwin, whose grandfather, a non-golfer, was the great evolutionist, author of *How to Prove the Survival of the Fittest Without being Actually Fit.* In 1956, in a Club match, Darwin had just become 2 up and 5 to play on me at Swinley Forest. I was pretty desperate and it seemed to me that some sort of Four might be attempted especially as it was justified by a recent incident in my family. Since we were old Club friends, we had never exchanged two words about personal affairs in thirty years acquaintanceship. It could jar the concentration of a normally sensitive man. I teed up my ball but before striking it I said:

'H.' (mentioning my wife), 'did extraordinarily well, yesterday, did you know? She's just produced a son.'

DARWIN: Actually it's my honour.

Darwin's technique was near perfect. The fact that,

even afterwards, he made no reference to my remark, made me feel as if I had been guilty of a hysterical outburst best soon forgotten.

But I have had a slight success with a minor branch of this gambit. It works best if your Opponent is your host or fellow-guest for the week-end. About the 3rd hole say:

'I wonder if I could ask you a bit of a favour?' Then stop short. It will 'plant a point of distraction'.

When my opponent was J. Abrahams, the well-known West Sussex cricketer famous for his hospitality, he waited four holes before he said:

'What was that you wanted to ask me?'

s.p.: Something quite fiddling. Wish I hadn't mentioned it. Tell you later.

If he asks you what's up yet once more, as Jack did about the 12th, say:

'Nothing. I simply wondered if you could be so frightfully kind as to do me a bit of a favour.'

ABRAHAMS: Oh yes, what sort of?

But I preferred to leave it to the 16th before I said: 'Yes, I wondered, could you possibly lend me a razor blade?'

No need to remind gamesmen that inflection is everything here. Opponent should be thinking in terms of being touched for at least a tenner. Reaction will affect his next drive.

Relief creates a tendency to pull.

7

WINNING PLAY

THIS may be a brief chapter. It is advice to the man who is, say, three up and eight to play. It is advice to the man who is on top, and gamesmanship's chief care is for the underdog.

Nevertheless there are tragic stories of gamesmen who, finding themselves 4 up and 7 to play even, have lost the match to a layman.* This is one of the real tragedies of the games world: and it should be the gamesman's task to examine the event with the courage and lack of self-deception without which no scientific advance is possible.

The *problem* of the winning golfer must be to win. He may be nervous of his 80-year-old head clerk, he may have to stand outside the dining room practising the tone of voice which he is going to use for saying 'good morning' to his twelve-year-old daughter; yet he must, even if he is as much as 8 up and 12 to play in a 36-holes match, have the courage to conquer. *Kill, kill,*

---

* Lawn Tennis shows equally painful examples. In the early rounds of the Davis Cup of 1967, Great Britain's representative lost 5 match points, thereby losing us the tie, against Eastern Ruthenia; equally the U.S. lost after leading against Petacatapopl, a mountain, in the Northern Andes.

kill – and only the gamesman will realize the courage involved, the bravery of the man who will beat his opponent even in a situation when there can be no one on earth, unless a gamesman be present, to say 'good shot'.

The *answer* to this problem is that any games player likes best to attack from behind. He can sometimes perform feats which were hitherto impossible to him. The crowd are on his side; women suddenly find him rather sweet. And the cause as we all know is a purely chemical one – secretion of adrenalin (or, in popular terms, $C_{10}H_{15}NO_3$).

If it has taken the science of gamesmanship to show that the man one down in the game is essentially one up in the manship, then gamesmanship must find the answer.

LIST OF SUGGESTED ADRENALIN DEPRESSANTS

Most winning men who end up by losing fail because they do not take advantage of their position.

At TWO UP it is possible to begin depression by *encouragement*. Start saying 'good shot', and use this phrase whenever your lay opponent hits a ball not absolutely off the extreme edge of the toe of the club. Practise saying it in an *increasingly mechanical* way. If layman's drive is on fairway say, 'You certainly powdered that one', even if it is 25 yards short of your own drive.

Note. Complimenting opponent on length of drive which is yet shorter than yours is a ploy which used to be advised only if gamesman was physically larger than lay opponent. How wrong we were! 'Buzzer' Swansby, at 5′ 1″, in this way thoroughly undermined the Rev.

'Hippo' Mingis,* who played full-back for Oxford 1935-7.

The effect of this can be increased if you have lost the honour and are driving second. Warmly compliment opponent on his shot, then shape up for your own with a sort of smiling confident bigness. No need to emphasize the absolute necessity, here, of driving your own ball 20–40 yards farther. This can be a killer especially if, after hitting what you know to be a good one, you follow the advice of Cardew and immediately stoop to pick up your tee and turn to your trolley to replace driver and carefully button up its head cover while your ball is still bouncing to a stop. I remember Tom Spicer, who specialized in analogies from fantastically ancient history, saying that this style 'reminded him of Vic'. Only I, who specialize in the history of ancient historical analogies, knew that this referred to Victor Trumper, of whom it was noted, when he batted for Australia against England round about 1902, that as soon as he struck the ball full, he was so certain it was going to be a boundary that he immediately turned on his heel and started chatting to the wicket keeper.†

The advantage of this 'good shot' irritant, is that it is difficult to counter. If layman attempts a reply it is not

* Pronounced 'Menzies'.

† 'This perfect analogy from cricket may not be fully enjoyed by American readers. We must wait for a more suitable hour to explain that the mere existence of cricket, the fabric and design of which is gamesmanship, meant that not only cricket but gamesmanship was first played in my country. All the more credit to the U.S., therefore, in having made the act of acceptance and taken their historic place in the international brotherhood of the gamesplay.'

(from a talk given to young people in Samothrace, Pa.)

likely to be effective. 'It wasn't really,' is feeble. 'No it wasn't, damn it,' pleases the gamesman because this proves his technique is telling.

'I can do much better than that, I assure you,' produces a great warm drone of a repeated 'I'm sure you can, I'm sure you can ...'

ADVICE AND ITS TIMING

Gamesman, having succeeded with his first tactic, will find that at THREE UP more than one new field is open to him.

During this period he must be particularly careful, in order to conceal his growing fright, to appear especially confident. Three-up therefore is the time when, little by little, the winning gamesman may give advice. Start by seeming to examine, at first casually, your man's swing. Then make brief pendulum-like motions with your left hand, as if you were taking a club through a quarter swing and correcting some fault you had noted in him. Later say (but the remark must burst out of you):

'D'y'know –'

Stop short as if you hadn't spoken. Opponent will suspect what's coming, and at the next hole you can start.

G.G.: May I say something?

O.: Ra-*ther*.

G.G.: You're not hitting it right on the meat, are you? It's not the usual sound your club makes. It's more a *schnoof!* than a *clock!* Are you doing that old business of forgetting to grip with the third and fourth fingers? –

(He starts to wiggle his finger.)
The third is the weakest finger.

This 'teach' approach is one of the most invulnerable attacks in gamesmanship. If next shot by layman is still weak, gamesman can say:

'You see?'

If it comes off he can use the 'good 'ittle boy, eat it up' tone to say, scoopingly:

'*That's* more like it.'

Now let us take this quite pleasant little technique a step further – and suddenly opponent should feel the touch of a chill wind. The one-upness or hubris of the winner should begin to extend beyond the realm of golf. Suddenly the one-down – now three- or FOUR-down – finds himself being lectured to *on his own subject*. Suppose Loser is an actor at present appearing in a Shakespeare play, winner may say, suddenly:

WINMAN: I haven't seen your *Much Ado About Nothing*.

LOSEMAN: Why don't you come along? It's quite an amusing production.

WINMAN: You're playing the lead?

LOSEMAN (*shifting his feet*): Yes, the conventional lead – Claudio.

WINMAN: Rather a pill of a part, isn't it? I mean, of all the unattractive bounders –

LOSEMAN: It's a challenge. He was a hero to the Elizabethan audience, of course.

WINMAN: *Really?* I'm surprised to hear you say that.

LOSEMAN (*sulkily*): Why?

WINMAN: Well, wasn't it a question of Shakespeare being interested in the Benedick–Beatrice relationship and dashing off the rest of the play just to fill in the gaps?

LOSEMAN: Not altogether.

When three-up becouse FOUR-UP Winman seems to feel that he can take it upon himself to advise not only on golf and life but on other *games*, particularly games which layman fancies. 'No, no, lock your wrists,' he will say, 'for that shot. If you played polo you'd know what I mean.' Soon Winman could be telling even an American opponent, a product of the Ivy League, what Van Breda Kolff did in basketball before he came to Princeton.

Finally Winman will be slipping into top, and telling you how to be natural with Effie, your own eight-year-old daughter, or describing the kind of nosegay a woman likes to be given when you take her out to dance, as if people really gave nosegays, and why she will think the Ponytail Room is out of date. When FOUR UP is stabilized Winman can make use of 'four-up friendliness' and be chatty and informal. An excellent subject for conversation would be that to-morrow, on Sunday, you have to play the semi-final of the Redwood Competition, and you are up against rather a hot man. Talk thus:

G.G.: Do you mind if I take a 3 iron on this tee?

O.: No. Why?

G.G.: This hole is very like the 15th at Snubbs Top, where I'm playing this match. And one's got to be straight as a rifle.

In other words this is just a practice round for me. The point can be prettily emphasized by carefully putting out each hole even after you have won it.

IMITATION FLUKE PLAY

When FIVE UP you will be nearly home, but the true gamesman will continue to attack till the finish. Let me remind the reader of an old gambit he might use here. Originally devised for the billiards table (1947) it consists in essence of an imitation fluke. A shot which in fact comes off as intended can have a deadly effect if it can be made to appear that its path was assisted by outside forces. If some dark power is ranged against him as well, Loseman is likely to give up altogether. Thus after a long drive say apologetically:

'Must have pitched on the path.' Or 'My ball on the green? It must have rebounded off the signpost.' Or (knowing well that it hasn't) 'Oh Lord, I'm afraid my drive must have just reached that devilishly well placed little pot bunker.'

ANTI-RECOVERY PLAY

In spite of all precautions, it does happen that even you, the gamesman, when seemingly in a winning position, will find your lead being eaten away. Suddenly 5 up becomes 1 up. The spectators, even if they are only two caddies and a terrier with a strong dash of King Charles's spaniel, will turn against you, and pro him. Women will glance shyly and smilingly in his direction. Once again, let reason and science be your guide. You will be certain to panic, and nothing can reverse that process: but for a most imperative reason you must learn how to appear calm at these moments. Learn to re-enact the positions and gestures associated

Practice indifference.

with indifference (practise is everything here). Praise your opponent's improved play, in a drawling voice, and then go off into a great haze of vagueness and relaxation.

The point of relaxed play is that opponent is bound to be under extra nervous strain, which will be intensified if gamesman seems unperturbed. It will be further increased if there are interruptions or distractions to which the player at such moments is particularly sensitive.

No gamesman will purposely go 'Boo' as the golfer is about to play; what he will do is to adopt the method perfected by Ronald Simpson in the war years of the forties. It has long been known as 'Simpson's Statue', first described by me in the *Atlantic Monthly* in the year Airborne won the Derby. The sequence is perfectly simple. The movement; the apology; the exaggerated freeze. The unnatural silence assumed by Simpson beautifully illustrated this fine old ploy.

'It is not the game that matters, it's the winning.'

This dict of gamesmanship could be broadened to include a hitherto neglected branch of golf play. Once again Gold Gamesmanship brings you a First in games analysis, however stumblingly.

HOW TO WIN THE WINNING

To win is a one-up situation if ever there was one. Yet how often, if one has won, does one find that somebody will come up to you and say 'Who won that thingummy in the end?'

'Well, as a matter of fact,' you start, but already your questioner is being plucked away by some girl who is cadging a drink. Or a young man in what looks like a wig may say:

'What were those people doing on the last green?'

If there is anybody watching, the established thing is to go over to the loser with a Big-Man smile, shake his hand easily* and say:

'Wonderful game, I had all the luck.'

---

* Though beware, loser may look at your hand as if he was wondering what it was there for, take it awkwardly as if he were good-humouredly taking part in a Patagonian ritual, and make you feel as if you were a walking parody of an all-too-British British.

There are many faults with this procedure. Firstly people on edge of group may be left unsure of the winner since loser could go through similar passes while smiling just as much as winner. Secondly loser will not only agree that you have had all the luck; he will be offended that you did not admit that the

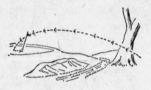

(a) *Path of ball to hole as winner of hole remembers it.*

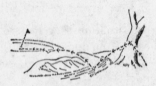

(b) *As it seemed to loser.*

number of flukey bounces you enjoyed makes nonsense of the laws of probability and proves the intervention of the Unknown. He will also believe he can beat you next time. We prefer one of the following procedures:

(a) With a putter tucked under arm, stand on green for a few moments and seem to concentrate on marking something up on your card. Then turn with a brief smile to your opponent and say 'Nice game'. This will make him feel out of it and that you belong to a higher world.

(*b*) Put on sentimental expression, tap opponent's elbow with an under arm bowling action and say quietly but meaninglessly 'You're on.' Then turn broadly smiling to friend or friends and never ever again mention luck.

(*c*) Do not say 'thanks for the game' but start talking to Loser in a warm and friendly way about something else altogether.

Try saying:

'What a good course – and what a beautiful one. I know the rhododendrons are nearly over, but when the leaves come into their own again – that's another victory.'

Loser will loathe anything poetical at this moment. He will also feel that this has just been a routine match for you, one of those early rounds in the competition.

ii. 'Phew, what a course! Every hole an intelligence test, every pitch a *viva* for First Class Honours.'

Having moved from the course to the club-house, Winner can evoke the atmosphere of *fading friendliness*. If women are present Winner can say to Loser, suddenly grave: 'Look, I want you to meet my wife.' Winner can then forget all about this and will be found by Loser, ten minutes later, talking amusingly to three women none of whom, obviously, is his wife. Loser wonders if he can go home.

If only men are present, Winner will say, 'Now the drinks are on me!' Again Loser will be standing on the edge of a group, and be eventually handed his drink – not the one he asked for – by Winner, who passes the glass backwards, still talking, and without looking round.

Loser will then go home, and Winner will immediately start talking about him.

'Afraid Wilkie was a little browned off –' etc.

8

A CHOICE FOR THE LOSEMAN

I BEGAN the last chapter with the statement that, in golf, one down was one up. The situation appeals to the fighting instinct: the brave horse, the real racer, likes to come up from behind.

Statistics prove that only 28.3 per cent of all golfers are brave, I hear the reader saying. Quite so: but this is where we must call on gamesmanship, and One-down must take his choice of the primaries and secondaries we have described, trying each in turn if necessary.*

But there are certain ploys, and in particular one gambit or group of ploys, which are especially suitable for the player who is trailing in the match. These I propose now to list.

Asking for instruction is certainly one of these. '*Why do I do something?*' say.

'Why do I miss a chip *completely*, sometimes?'

It takes a Seligmann to answer 'Can't think', in the tone of voice of a man saying 'keep your trap shut'. The average player cannot help saying – 'I think you must remember to *swing* – just swing – and don't try to knock it *up*: the loft will do that.'

Perfectly correct advice but when your two-up opponent is faced with this shot himself he is bound to

---

* In the old days, so much more amusing, of mixed gamesmanship styles, I remember little Pip von Steiler changing from 'he's so amazingly fit' (the Always In Training ploy) to the 'he's probably in considerable pain' during the same match.

think of it fractionally as a show-you-how shot and be affected by the law that turns nearly all demonstration shots into missed shots, even if they are performed before an almost idiotically young grandchild. *Loseman must make him make the unconscious conscious.*

IT'S MY TEMPO *v.* YOUR TEMPO...

There are times when the playing of the game and the playing of the gamesmanship almost merge.

A good but neglected rule in all matches except team games is PLAY YOUR OWN TEMPO. Do not fall into the trap of unconsciously imitating the rhythm of your opponent. I am not going to tell the story of how Peter Baverstock got through three rounds of the Rusper and Angmering Croquet Vase by trotting between each stroke. There was a lot of laughter and the whole thing may have been rigged up. But slow play *v.* fast play is a common contest round the billiard table.

If Scatter annoyed Rimming by being over deliberate at golf, he sent him into a real frenzy in the snooker game after tea. He would (a) suddenly realize, late, it was his turn; (b) survery the scene; (c) practically kneel down to align the white; (d) go up to the other end of the table to do the same thing with some miscellaneous reds as if he was planning a large break; (e) take 8 practise swings before (g) missing the object ball altogether.

Nor does it have to be a still ball game. The day before writing these words (July '67) I was at Wimbledon watching the dramatic defeat, on the first day, of the singles champion Santana by the unseeded American Passarell. No single report this morning gives the real reason for the defeat – that Passarell moved more slowly to take up his position after the rally was completed. If Santana had been a fine gamesman instead of just a fine player he might have done his part by staring whimsically at the sky as he waited, or sitting on his up-turned racket.

In golf, 'my tempo *v.* yours' is a valuable gambit. A. should be slow if B. is fast, and vice versa. A. should emphasize the nerve play of his slowness over detail when the detail is of no practical use, e.g., if he is on the lip of a little bank behind a brook over which he has to play towards the green, he should examine the brook closely and possibly – though this may seem exaggerated – he may think of putting his finger in the brook to test its temperature.

At a later hole he may be particularly deliberate over his second shot if couple behind is waiting to drive and, after shaping up for shot change his mind about which club to use – perhaps putting his number 4 back in the bag and taking it out again.

B.'s ploy is to carry his speeding-up style to the confines of, but not as far as, bad etiquette. He must start walking forward immediately. A. starts his downswing. Whenever he has to wait, he will emphasize the fact by unfolding his shooting stick with a thoroughness and deliberation suggestive of pitching camp.

I always see this particular gambit in terms of the personalities of Rimming and Scatter, who embodied so many aspects of it in their forty years battle.

THERE ARE THINGS MORE IMPORTANT THAN GOLF

This phrase sums up the major gambit of the one-down, in golf. Loseman MUST try to weaken his

B. in play against A. (p. 107)

opponent and minimize the game by suggesting that, for Heaven's sake, there are other things in the world besides swinging a golf club.

LAST UP EVEREST

This is a ploy which was much in use in the forties but is now almost completely outmoded and I mention it now as an interesting curiosity. The loseman starts talking about 'loving golf', which he 'wants to play seriously'. He then goes on to say that he's 'finished with mountain climbing in the Himalayas' or that, he's 'got to face it, there's no more rowing for me, the doctors say.'

'That year, rowing at Henley,' (I remember Saxe saying) 'I displaced my heart nine inches, apparently.'

'Where to?' said Odoreida.

'They recommended golf,' said Saxe, taking no notice.

In the old days when gamesmanship was less widely known, this kind of approach could impress the completely novice layman and, though this seems unlikely now, would take the edge off his offensive spirit.

WHERE'S THE TELEPHONE

The suggestion that work is more important than games is not regarded as a tenable gambit if the game is golf; yet some have gone to great lengths to try and retrieve their general status by references to 'my call to Amsterdam' and have even hired men to 'find them at all costs somewhere on the course' with a message or merely to say in an overheard whisper, 'The Shop says not to touch it, sir.' Gattling-Fenn was particularly

Another message for Gattling

persistent in this habit, persuading a very old brother-in-law of his to do the trick in return for a ticket for a Yeovil football match.

Gattling's ploy became a sort of joke with us: but Gattling was over 60 now, so we made a pact not to rag him.

WHERE WAS MCCLELLAN AT THE
BATTLE OF THUNDER RUN?

Business talk of the 'City' kind is in fact too like school and thought to be best not mentioned. Something to do with the Arts however is much more respected especially by people who generally talk business. In a 4-ball at Beaconsdale, Virginia, we were four down against Dowell and Cussman, two Southerners. Suddenly my partner from England, Johnny Page, got on top of a bunker and made a picture frame with his hands. Even I did not know what was coming.

'We're filming a reconstruction of May 8th 1864,' said Page. 'You know – McClellan's Disaster.'

'But he never had a disaster,' said Cussman.

'Well, he did in a *sense*,' said Dowell.

Soon the argument between them raged, and as this gave place to mutual recrimination, the desire and ability to hold their lead against us faded.

If anxiety about telephone messages is to be used at all, betting should be the simulated cause. Few golf-playing men like to admit to having no interest in horse racing. Most of them would like to speak the language. If their opponent makes a dash for the club telephone whenever windings of the course make this possible, a glimpse of the gaudy world of gambling adds a touch of glamour to the day.

'Cardew's off,' they say.

'He got one-two-three on the Selling Plate at Sandown yesterday, apparently.'

Cardew had nothing of the kind, I happened to know: but the fact that he was secretive about his betting made newcomers talk of large sums passing hands; though I don't suppose Cardew ever stood to lose more

than five shillings in his life, and 'popping in to telephone' often only meant, in cold weather, a small rum
and orange at the bar. I suspect that this 'secret' betting of Cardew's would not have been so effective a
ploy if Cardew hadn't been the best golfer of our
bunch, a genuine mid-seventies man.

LATER HISTORY OF THE NATURAL HISTORY GAMBITS

'And what about the *Natural History Gambits?*' my
few surviving gamesmen friends will be saying.

In those days, if 4 down against an opponent who
knew nothing about nature, we used to stop and pick
some old bit of grass.

'False bearded holosteum!' we used to say to lay
opponents, as if we were sharers of some joy from par-
ticipation in which Fate had banned him. Gilbert Saxe
used to add a touch of *misplaced poetry*.

'Humble, now,' I once heard him say at Frilford,
looking at a sort of messy rosette. 'But in a month's
time at Easter time the pasque flower. The "bloom
Pascal",' he added in a rather churchy way. Carraway
was our fourth and he was sensitive to religious atmosphere. His drive at the next hole just caught the top of
the cross bunker.

New golf courses, often undeliberately, retain rare
flowers in the rough, especially in Spain, a country,
incidentally, where the slightest interest in wild flowers
is met, by visitors and inhabitants alike, with the cold
and secretly curious glance reserved for people who
have been psycho-analysed. A variation on the 'Stop!
Look at this!' nature ploy was, however, tried on us by
the American manager at Sotto Grande. He was telling

me about how at last they had found the right fairway covering and talking to me particularly because earlier in the round I had done my old business, when my ball went into the rough, of picking a leaf and saying: 'I didn't know bristle agrostis grew here!'

'This is our grass for the fairways,' Al went on.

'Ah,' I said, turning to Saxe, who had come to Spain for the bridge. 'Turf cut from the downs above Chanctonbury?'

'How do you mean?' said the Manager.

' "Close, sheep-bitten, west-wind worn"?' Saxe murmured.

'How's that again? No – here we are. Look.' The expert stooped and picked up a fresh divot.

'Look at this,' he said.

'What?' I said.

'It's taken us three years and we shall improve on it. You know grasses. Get it?'

Was I holding the bit of turf upside down?

701   702

'Rye 702 and bluegrass G in equal quantities.'

'702?' I said, but Al dismissed the subject. Obviously he thought I couldn't even recognize rye as a genus, which in fact I can. But better to shut up, I thought, three-putting.

Modern gamesmanship has forged sharper natural history gambits than this for the competitor who is, say, over one down with less than ten to play.

Young Reggie Cornpetter (9) was doing biology at Basingstoke, and he was a great believer in suddenly mentioning geology. Playing with Reggie at Liphook, Hampshire, I would unexpectedly find my ball on one of the lower holes beyond the road, bogged down in clay.

'Look,' I would say.

'Typical of the Weald,' says Reggie. 'You never know when you're going to strike clay.'

We had to warn strangers not to say 'why' to Reggie. But I was amused when, playing at Mildenhall with Reggie and Saxe, Saxe's ball frequently came to rest on that strip of sand which meanders through the course. It was bad luck.

'Where's it come from?' said Saxe.

'It's recent,' said R.C.

'Then it ought to be marked "Ground under repair".'

'No, no,' said R.C. 'I mean "recent" in the geological sense. Less than thirty million years old.'

Saxe was going to answer 'High time it was dealt with' but I nudged him.

Until Dowland-Smith joined our 4-ball, Reggie continued to do well with geology. If I were his opponent, at Chelmsford, and had to play an awkward hanging lie, Reggie would say:

REGGIE: Nasty lie.

S.P.: Yes.

REGGIE: Typical glaciated scenery.

Reg knew I knew this one, but he would address my partner.

'You see these slopes are literally *gouged* out by a glacier, a huge block of ice about a mile thick.'

Believe it or not I had exactly the same sort of lie for my third shot as well.

'Oh yes,' said Reg Cornpetter. 'Typical of Essex. You get the same thing in Upper New York. The lakes. Gouged out. Hallo – head up!'*

THE BALTUSROL

Ploys may come and ploys may go, and if one gets over-used another comes along to take its place. In the end we learned how to manage Reggie: and quick as a flash Dowland-Smith came along with a new nerve tester, one which was only vaguely connected with natural history but useful, I would say, for a sudden shock if your opponent is one up and one to play.

It is called the Baltusrol gambit after the famous golf-course in New Jersey, scene of 1967's National Open. Nicklaus played with Palmer and it has been whispered to me that Palmer used this fine local ploy against Nicklaus on the 18th tee. Nicklaus, shaken,

---

* Though I had scuffed the shot it was not of course because of 'head up'; but Reggie was quite right to repeat this, automatically, for a miss, though it is better just to say 'OO' sharply, for a top, until the player hears this 'oo' in his head *before his club hits the ball.*

wisely took a 2 iron instead of his driver at the final hole. But first I must explain the gambit.

Baltusrol is named after a famous murder committed within its precincts; and 'the Dowland-Smith' consists, very simply, in suggesting some part of a golf course is of ill omen. Smith, of Nettlebed, Oxon., had a very long nose which he thought of as keen like Sherlock Holmes's. Driving out of London he would start to create the atmosphere by taking the route down Du Cane Road past Wormwood Scrubbs Prison.

'Du Cane was the famous prison reformer,' he said.

'. . . well, when we say reformer . . .' he went on and then stopping at the end of Glanders Road he would ask his opponent to look at No. 2.

'The other half of the body was never found,' he would say.

Then the game started on the Huntercombe course – 'outwardly so beautiful', Smith would say. 'This is where they found the signalman's foot.'

Last time I was playing with him he kept his crime to the 14th, where it is fatal to hook.

'Do you see that shadow beyond the green?' he said. 'That is your line . . . rather interesting, it's where they found a bloodstained pram. In broad daylight. Just left there. That was 1928. Some say that it was left in the middle of the green, standing quite solitary, in the sunshine. But there's shadow now.'

I am told that Nicklaus drove with his iron because Palmer had murmured to him that on that tree on the left they found the old doctor where the Indian had left him hanging. Hanging by the feet. He had been there some time.

What has been at the back of my mind all this time? What scene has fascinated me since I first began to play golf? As we set off for the far holes of the beautiful Isle of Purbeck course, we are on the heath, where twilight seems to come earlier, as Hardy says. Across this Heath, Edgon Heath, the native returned, and one can hear the wind in the thorn as Hardy described it. Some say that it was on this heath that King Lear went mad.

'What do you think?' I asked Saxe. His ball was trapped in the blackened roots of the heather.

'Edward the Seventh said he thought this was the best view in England,' said Saxe, always keen to quote royalty. But he hadn't got the point. He put his second bang in the middle of the green.

9

CLUB-HOUSE PLAY

'The Secret of Clubhouse Play is timing.'
J. Castelnau Greene

CHANGING-ROOM BLUES

FOR many of us, golf gamesmanship starts in the changing-room of the club-house. Let us say there has been no pre-play build up, no journey down with your opponent to the course. Maybe you have both of you cut away early from work on a summer evening. How delightful to be peeling off gloomy office clothes, with their miserable appearance of wrinkled smartness, and getting into good old golf slacks.

Yet is it possible for a man to enter a changing-room without a tremor, particularly if he is about to play a club match, however minor? Most boys suffer pangs of nervousness when changing for a school football match or for college rowing. Buried traces of this remain in manhood. Images of old pieces of yellow soap or lockers with broken hinges keep floating to the surface from the subconscious. How easy for the gamesman to summon up that changing-room nervousness once more.

'Good, we'll just make it,' he may say. Make *what* doesn't matter.

Or he may, by simply being ready first, just stand and stare at his man who finds himself in consequence (*a*) changing more hurriedly than necessary, (*b*) trying to cover up torn and twisted old underpants, (*c*) forgetting to bring onto the course his packet of gum.

CLUB SECRETARY PLAY

Alternatively, gamesman can say:

'Hallo! The Secretary's on the first tee. What's he up to?'

In Britain, the secretary is often a retired Army officer, who may be Old Foggibags to the Chairman of the club, but to a non-committee man or junior member he is an object causing secret uneasiness, which in the main is what secretaries are for.

My advice to Golf Secretaries is that they should be either (*a*) friendly or (*b*) unpleasant. There must be nothing in between, though I have known type (*a*) to switch to (*b*) overnight. 'Friendly' is generally not too efficient but spreads the impression that he is popular,

and in fact he is popular even though it is known that he is so frightened of Mrs Billow, in charge of teas and sandwich luncheons, that he cannot interview her without first having a Scotch.

But a far more gamesmanlike atmosphere is evoked

if the secretary is bossy, irritable and clear cut. In his
private life he is a timid parent, a respected husband
and an uncle who knows when to keep his mouth shut.
Even when playing golf on his own golf course he is
diffident and prone to apologize. But on club premises
he seems to be always waiting to pounce. Softwood
boards are pinned full of notices all signed in his un-
characteristically flowing hand. Outside, a

KEEP THIS PATH CLEAR OF
TROLLEYS

notice, signed J. Eldon Swing, Hon. Sec., is the first
thing you see outside the club. A few steps farther
and

NO ENTRANCE

is half hidden behind a rather more prettily typed
announcement in Gill Sans:

DOGS ABSOLUTELY PROHIBITED

and if you try to get your spaniel out of the car for a
run (actually its gait is a kind of sea-lion waddle) along
the ditch by the boundary, the secretary will be out in
a second, sharp, small:

'I say, do you mind?'

Major Swing is a typical secretary of this kind. Modest in manner, he will in print shout at the top of his
voice. Even as we enter we stop dead:

NO NAILED SHOES BEYOND
THIS DOOR

A new confused member may feel that he must enter
barefoot, if beyond the notice he sees the worm-eaten

remains of some unrecognizable floor covering. There is no doubt that a keep-you-on-your-toes secretary, by increasing the tension, helps to prepare the gamesfield.

ATTITUDE TO GUEST

This is particularly important if your opponent is your guest and is visiting your club for first time. In the bar, there are a number of routine tests which may be applied. First of all there is the question of standing drinks. If guest is the only non-member in the four-ball, is he stood drinks by his three opponents in turn? Probably – but what about 'his round'? Can he, not a member of the Club, order drinks at bar? Mightn't he be breaking a rule (like not raising your hat to something or other in the march past)? What is the alternative? To look stuffy and do nothing while the other three edge away from him?

An awkward choice – and gamesman can make sure guest takes the wrong decision.

But already host may have undermined guest by the gambit of wrong clothesmanship, particularly if guest prides himself on his rather trad clothes – a specially cut scarf designed for wearing instead of a tie. A woollen jacket made without a lapel. Of course I said nothing about scarves when I led my guest to the bar.

'Excuse me, sir.'

The steward spoke to me very quietly, after doing the drinks.

'Yes, Mason?' I said loudly. 'What is it?'

Mason lowered his voice still further.

'Your guest, sir. No tie.'

'Quite, quite, quite,' I said. 'So sorry, so sorry, so sorry.' I drew aside my guest who happened to be A.J.S.

stealing his first day from work this summer. The scarf was new, subdued, well tied.

'A.J.' I said, very quietly indeed. 'Awfully sorry. Ridiculous rule –' then I patted my Adam's apple.

no tie

'Tie,' I said. A.J.S. did have an old ragged tie in his bag, which happened to be salmon coloured, and indeed pink – impossible not to notice. I knew it was the exclusive Leander Club tie but Cosmo Tickler whispered something behind A.J.'s back.

'Trade Unions are the most ...' I heard. The most what? 'But unofficial strikes are – well....'

I once nearly scored a fine double with this routine, getting Coad with the tie ploy and then at lunch time pulling the leg of P.B.N., who was then our Ambassador at The Hague.

Playing on the hottest day of 1947 I managed to shepherd him into the club-house dining-room before our game. He was wearing a white tropical suit with half-length sleeves. Within 30 seconds Major Swing's shiny bald head rose from a corner table and he was by our side.

'Sorry,' he started.

'May I introduce His Excellency –' I began, in a

super-courtly manner, thinking Swing might know P.B.'s name or be cowed by the H.E.

'Sorry,' he repeated. 'We have a rule about jackets in the luncheon room.'

If only P.B. had protested, but to my disappointment he just laughed, patted me on the back and said, 'I'm sorry but it's hopeless to try to dress up to the sartorial standard of my host,' – putting me one down.

But Coad, involved in the tie incident, started his afternoon round with an air shot.

TRANSATLANTIC GUEST PLAY

Every American golfer has his own story about the English golf club-house: and every Englishman who plays in America is able to establish his one-upness as a man who succeeded in having run the gauntlet of the American equivalent. In the Paradise Valley Country Club he was once 'lost somewhere between the cinema and the Turkish Baths'.

In the shower room, 'the towel and slippers they give you are burnt after use' (you can tell the story) 'and it isn't only mine they burn either'. Faced with this one-down situation, the Englishman in Arizona may express naïve and rather charming surprise as if it was his first experience of luxury. He may tell tall stories of Club life in Britain, members at lunch not daring to ask for more, etc. Another school of British thought may take a different line altogether. Never be surprised, is their rule. Never comment either; except that, after a time, you start to criticize. It is the hygiene you criticize. Suspiciously, you look hard at the snowy pile of bath towels, ready folded for use near the infra-red machines.

'*That's* never been estered,' you say, poking a finger into one of them.

'Estered?' they say.

'Estered or esterized,' you say. 'You see, unless the tiny microscopic filaments of the wool plastic are sheathed in the estering dymogin, their condition cannot be 100 per cent clean.'

'How's that?'

'I hope this is new, this towel?'

'I've found piles of bath towels left like this. With a pocket glass you can see that their undersides are a tangle of *tricium*. It has a smell, not completely unpleasant, rather like barley.' *Take up towel and sniff.*

Another problem occurs when the Englishman returns the hospitality in his own country. Shall he scour the countryside for a club-house changing-room which contains a weighing machine, two showers and a man who sometimes takes mud off shoes? No – quite wrong. Have special English Way of Life showpiece genuine old washbasin with either a hole where the hot tap should be, or a tap which belches air, coughs and drizzles before actually producing warm water. Show American guest a row of pre-war nail brushes, each one tightly chained to the surface ('Can't be too careful ... Lots of robberies here ... big nailbrush raid last Spring'). Show him old socks, odd, undarned piled under a PLEASE DO NOT TOUCH notice.

'Yes I know,' say. 'I know you do things much more antiseptically in the States; but we always think that unless there's some dirt about it's hard to make really good gravy.'

WORK OF COSMO TICKLER

Either England, or America, has the reputation, in America, or England, of being tremendously well-behaved and gentlemanly in club-houses. In the famous America Sports Club which admitted me (this was before the affair of '32) as a temporary member, I remember staring hard into the face of a club man who looked so absolutely gentlemanly that even I doubted my capacity to compete.* At the same time it may interest Americans to know that we have in this country† men who are not gentlemanly at all but whose manners on the contrary are rather caddish; stranger still, this caddishness *is a gambit*.

We have said already something of the insensitiveness of Cosmo Tickler. So far as clothesmanship was concerned, he did admirably by parodying the whole thing. He would wear pink plus fours with a violet shirt, in the mixed bar at Sunningdale.

'Mind if I strip to the waist?' he would say, and actually take his tie off and undo two shirt buttons. As a visitor to Cypress Point, it is said that he stood in the doorway of the Members Only section and executed a

---

* A few minutes after this contest the American, a retired investor, fell forward on his face and was carried out by an even more gentlemanly attendant.

† and sometimes in the States. But certain young golfers of *what* nation was Alistair Cooke describing as a 'cross between a gorilla and a musical comedy'?

little step dance as if asking for an invitation to come in. Then when nobody raised their heads:

'Is "Big-end" Cardington here today?' He spoke in a clear throaty tenor. One member is believed to have smiled, rather liking to learn this nickname of an unpopular trustee, to whom the Club owed 50,000 dollars.

There are legends about Cosmo which I am pretty certain are untrue. One is that when he played at Sunningdale on a warm day with Cyril Climping, Chairman of the Society for the Preservation of Lawns, as his partner, the Opposition bribed Cosmo to 'behave impossibly'. Near the 3rd, on the Old, which runs parallel to the Ladies Course, if he saw, say, the Lady Captain of the Berkshire, playing with the Comtesse de Saint Sauveur, he might give them a wolf whistle and, when they turned their heads, go through the motions of pretending to spray himself with deodorant.

But I shall always think of Cosmo Tickler as, basically, a specialist in Advanced Club-house.

Perhaps this is the place to record another gambit parallel to, but oh so different from, Cosmo's hard joke approach. I mention it with reluctance. It must be dealt with delicately. But everybody knows now that Gattling-Fenn, as he got older, became quite simply a rude joke merchant – I mean he used jokes of the kind which the ladies, retired to the drawing-room to exchange unspeakable secrets, imagine, usually quite wrongly, are being bandied about by the gentlemen round their port. If one was talking about where to go for holidays, almost every place name one chose would cause Gattling to glaze his eyes as if he found the proper names improper in some way. Perfectly ordi-

nary phrases like the Costa Brava or Fez or Corsica or
the Leaning Tower of Pisa, particularly the last two,
would set Gattling off on one of his slow high giggles.
And the amazing thing was that this habit of Gattling's
started one looking for dirty meanings in the most
innocent remarks oneself, and rather enjoying doing
so. Needless to say Gattling used his habit all the time
on the golf course. Golf scoring became particularly
complex and irritating if he was present. We got bored,
and one day Boyce said he was going to 'nip Gattling
in the bud'.

Wondering idiotically if there wasn't something
peculiar about that phrase too, I waited with interest
to see what Boyce would do. It was a parlay, in form.

'Now, Gattling,' he said, when we had got back to
the tea room and Gattling was speechless with laughter
at some hidden joke which only he had seen. 'You
obviously saw some joke which we didn't. What was
it?'

'I don't want to embarrass you, old man,' said
Gattling.

'I *am* embarrassed,' said Boyce. '*For you*. Do you
know why you make that kind of joke?'

'Search me,' said Gattling.

'It's simply that if you make sex jokes all the time it's
because you are *sexually suppressed*.'

Well done Boyce, I thought. But Gattling wasn't one
of the old originals for nothing.

'Me?' he said at the top of his voice. 'I'm the most sex
starved man in Bucks – WHOOF!' he called out, pretending to make a grab at Elsie, aged 46, our waitress,
who was delighted. 'But –'

(At this point Gattling lowered his voice and, looking intently at Boyce, added):

'But I never expected to be told so by an inhibited masochistic ectomorph.'

Boyce made the mistake of saying 'No I'm not'. The giggle started again, like the bleeps of a geiger counter.

TRAGEDY OF WIFFLEY

Let us finish with an incident in the history of club-house play which, undramatic as it is, shows its wide influence, and its use in the hands of an adherent to gamesmanship of only very modest competence.

Who, in ordinary circumstances, would have remembered Wiffley (16)? A buttoned-up little man, a round moustache on top of a small humourless face, his hair and clothes irritatingly neat, this unromantic figure yet had one thing in common with Byron – nobody knew his Christian name.

There was something so colourless about his play off the tee that very few people could remember his surname either.

'Excuse me Mr – er –'

The following incident, so important in Wiffley's life, happened casually. In the bar somebody was actually speaking to him.

'We're trying this pro-amateur match here next week. There may be a bit of a crowd. We wondered if you'd like to look after the 3rd hole.'

Wiffley could scarcely believe it.

'Why of course I –'

'You'd be a marshall, really.' It was the competition secretary. 'If you wouldn't mind making yourself into a sub-committee of one!'

This is the phrase which was the real turning point in Wiffley's life. The very word 'committee' sent tingles down Wiffley's spine. Now he, Wiffley, though not of course actually on the Committee, was to be an associate. It so happened that on the day of the golf match it rained steadily and the spectators were thinned out to three or four a match: but Wiffley followed each couple down the fairway of the 3rd from second shot to green holding a flag as if it were a torch and

actually signalling with it, before he trotted back to join the couple behind.

After this event Wiffley straightened up, tidied up and began talking in a new voice, rather firm.

'Heating O.K. in here?' he would say as he walked into the shower room.

A man drying himself stopped and wrapped the bath towel closer. His eyes narrowed.

Later, as Wiffley grew more confident, he began using the pronoun 'we'.

'How do you like the grass between the bunkers on the 15th?' he would say.

'Grass?' said Saxe, looking thoughtfully for a quotation. 'Grass, leaves of?'

'Turf.'

'How do you mean? Beneath this sod?'

'We've transferred it from the practise ground. I believe it's what we've been looking for.'

By purest chance I knew that Wiffley got this phrase from an old number of *Inland Golf*. But what initiative! This wasn't the Wiffley of the old days. This was the day Elsie, our tea waitress, smiled at him when she said, 'I'm sorry, crumpets are off.'

Sometimes he would walk up to the noticeboard and, frowning, scribble something on an envelope. Or I have seen him suddenly open the door of a cupboard which was full of old shoes, look hard and then shut it with a bang.

Ten years later, though he had still not received that call to be a member of committee which, in a tiny part of him, he expected, he would still look as if he knew just that little bit more than the average. Occasionally he would give the suspicion of a smile to old Sockington the Secretary, though he never spoke to him.*

* There are quite brutal ways of countering the Committeeman Gambit, but while Wiffley is alive I am unwilling to reveal them in the public print.

10

SPECTATORSHIP

ORIGIN OF EXPERT GAMES WATCHING

THE origin of Sports spectatorship will never be known till we have mastered the secrets of the Cretan vase tombs. All that we can do here is to suggest a graph of determinable progress.

In the earliest history of Scottish golf, gamesmanship was certainly used by spectator sportsmen who hung around a match in order to make bets in a carrying voice within earshot of selected competitors about to play their shots. A shout of 'Forty-five to one against', overheard on the first tee, can diminish the chances of the competitor who didn't want to play much anyhow.

There have been many isolated attempts to influence golf matches from the ring-side. The mere fact that the basic etiquette of the game insists on dead silence all round was itself a challenge to such men as Odoreida, who liked following a match which scarcely anyone else was watching. He went in for the No Reaction Whatever ploy – so that whether one laid a chip dead, or topped it 60 yards over the green, he would look blank. This somehow suggested that he had detected some mistake in your style so vital that nothing he could say would cure it. Mesmerized, I myself found my eyes wandering towards him after every shot I played.

I know that as a young man Odoreida's spectator

methods were more primitive. He would not actually talk on the stroke, but he would use his trick of unpleasant mimicry. While a player was almost finishing his putting routine – taking his last slow look – Odoreida would produce the faint cockney caw of a hen. Or he once distracted Holderton, son of Lord Holderton. Holderton was putting to save the match on the 18th (actually the 9th) in the semi-final of the President's Putter at Rye, and Odoreida, just below the brow of the hilltop tee of the 1st, made a sound like a nightingale. This, he told us later, was because Holderton was a naturalist and would know that, according to the text-books, a nightingale apparently would not be expected to be on this golf course, especially in January. On another occasion, when 3 down at Aberdovey, he suddenly disappeared into the long grass along the railway by the 6th. A moment later the sound of a baby crying was heard.

'That thing shouldn't be here,' said Cornpetter, irritated. Instantly Odoreida put his head up.

'It happens to be my nephew, sir,' he said. It was the only time Cornpetter was known to apologize.

Primitive ways of getting best view began to be studied. Some may remember the first appearance on the competition course of one or two men who wore armbands with a small red cross, and how these men stepped through the crowd, and stood quite near the players, unquestioned. These arm bands, originally in good material, were supplied by our Organization and on one occasion we experimented with a borrowed ambulance which conveyed respected older gamesmen half-way round the course before it was asked to 'show credentials'. Fortunately Gattling-Fenn, the spokesman, was there to act as spokesman.

'There are no credentials of blood transfusion, I believe,' he said. There was a pause.

'No affidavits of coronary occlusion,' he went on. 'No charter against the mending of a wound.' Later three officials apologized and one referee resigned.

In his later years Odoreida was able to go where he liked simply by wearing a walkie-talkie on his back. It was annoying, especially if one knew it was made of cardboard.

Spectators can actually be used by gamesmen as a means of influencing play. Let the competitor be clear about his own tendencies. Are you certain how you yourself react to onlookers? Neither one thing nor the other? Then make sure that when you play Oldmaster in the knock-out – Oldmaster who plays every course as if it were a public meeting and makes shouting conversation with embarrassed acquaintances on the next fairway – be sure you will choose a time when, ideally, the rest of the Club is at the wedding of the daughter of the popular Secretary. This will baffle Oldmaster. He will be looking round for audience and will end by talking to *you*, as if you were a crowd of twenty. Here is the time when, as never before, you must take no notice of him. Pretend you have nothing to do with him. Look at your watch. Make a note. This naturally works well with a lot of games besides golf. The law has offshoots. If Oldmaster played the first 9 holes well and a spectator appeared at the 9th, I would make no reference whatever to Oldmaster's previous good play. This would make Oldmaster feel that he had to prove himself all over again – thus putting a strain on the psyche. Remember here, as so often in gamesmanship and lifemanship, that the closer the parallel to life, the more penetrating the ploy.

The name of Oldmaster reminds me again of my old friend Gattling, who in later life became an exponent of misplaced heartiness and the unwelcome joke. In the golf club snooker room, it was Gattling who used to say, if one was shaping up to pot the pink:

'Down with the baby's bottom.'

And he would say it *every* time. As a golf spectator Gattling would use the same kind of language.

'Advancing by easy stages?' he would say, if one of us were playing his fifth to the green. Or if a second putt was missed a chanting voice would seem to be saying:

'And-a-three-and-a-fower-and-a-five-and-a-six.'

I mention this here because once Oldmaster, when we were playing and Gattling was doing his stuff, got back on me, by saying:

'Won't you introduce us to your friend?' Visitors looked at me intently.

Another peculiar example of Spectator Put-off is to be found in the recently reported case of the Flapping Plastic Mac. Two young professionals were in the throes of a needle match. One of them had an unusually pretty girl friend who wore a bright yellow mac. It was a squally day and this mac always seemed to be flapping (when he chipped or putted) within the vision of girl's boy friend's opponent, who suspected a plot, looked irritated and waited till the breeze dropped before making his shot. What are the rights of the thing? T. Rattigan believes that this is a case when players should not wait for weather conditions to change in their favour. We have been swamped with questions at H.Q. but it is too early to make a final ruling.*

* Many will remember little Wiffley and his hay fever. This was perfectly genuine, but it could be pretty hellish for his opponent

A SPECTATOR'S CHARTER

The use of spectators as an adjunct to games winning is scarcely a subject for a serious manual. Where it is believed that we can help is in the development of our organization for the improvement of the status of that great army of spectators who watch large professional golf tournaments. As most golfers know, there is a World Organization of Golf Gamesmen, and I have accepted their unspoken request that I should draw up a first charter acceptable not only to W.O.G.G. but to all those patient thousands of mid-eighties people who spend their leisure toiling round in respectful attendance and self-abnegating support while the high sixties people play their own peculiar form of golf.

SPECTATOR STATUS

Our first aim has been improvement of status. Hitherto all rules for spectators have been a series of Don'ts combined with a succession of Take Cares. Don't stroll about in bunkers. Don't run across the fairway. Don't talk, don't take photographs, don't bring performing dogs. This must be broken. Spectators should be encouraged to think positively, and to realize that there are certain things they can do, and most effec-

---

between 2 and 22 June, when the Timothy grass, his special allergy, was pollinating. He had a disyllabic sneeze, a low sharp RAH followed by a long high cooing OO – typical hay fever. When Opponent was playing he smothered it all with his handkerchief: but when he was playing himself he had to wait for a sneeze – then play quickly. Was it a sort of embryonic pity which put off all (except Odoreida) of Wiffley's opponents? That long exhausted 'ooo' stuck in the mind for days.

tively. Not only are golf watchers the only spectators who are themselves taking exercise: they can and must use initiative as well.

Spectator clothes are important and need experienced guidance. I do not say this because of the huge chain of sportswear shops with which I may be asked to associate my name. It is because once more, as in the old days, *spectators should be better dressed than*

Recommended spectator wear for
Englishman (left) and American (right).

players. We may return to this subject later. Let us just say, here, that the basic rule is not to be too informal, not too sporty and relaxed, unless your tailor is an experienced relaxed clothes specialist. In England a man at the height of summer won a public rebuke in a famous Sunday paper by taking off his shirt and planting himself on a vantage point by a short hole *wearing a string vest*. Do not, in America, wear bush shirt and trousers in boldly disharmonious colours. This may be correct for scratch men but fifteen-plus men should dress older than their age and think in terms of handsome well cropped characters with the vital grey moustaches and courteous eyes of male models in a whiskey advertisement.

BE A BORN LEADER

If you can achieve even only the very slightest appearance of distinction, many gambits are open to you. The ambitious spectator leader must not expect at once to make his mark on a P.G.A. tournament, or become the toast of Telstar. He should start with lesser competitions, and smaller crowds. Begin, perhaps, by tackling the novice spectator who allows himself to get excited about the number of dollars which, at later holes 'hang on that putt'.

NOVICE: This putt for five grand.

'Yes,' you say. 'And that, I suppose, means an average loss of two.'

'How do you mean?'

'Simply that these men are working for next to nothing – or rather for a deliberate capital diminution.'

'But Sykes – surely he's –'

'Work it out. No strategic financial reserve. No safeguard of convertible risk.'

Having suggested that you yourself are a little more well founded, one would hope, than the Player/Palmer outfit, you talk of a proposed fund for that great basic body of the professionals 'who entertain us for next to nothing'.

HOW TO KNOW THE RULES

An alternative gambit, which needs less bravura but more solid homework, is Knowledge of the Rules. Carry a copy of the Rules of Golf, preferably in a waterproof envelope. If any moot point occurs, even if it is merely a question of order of play, who's putt, etc., stand in commanding position, take book from envelope, find a place, look puzzled, shut book, put it back in envelope again. You yourself make no comment, but a few will glance at you interestedly.

Having established your position as a potential leader, even if no possible kind of rule has been called into question, you can yet heighten your standing with the small group likely now to be following you, by pointing out an alleged inadequacy in the rules book.

'Who is playing this game and who is not?' you can say for a start. 'See here,' you say, quoting. 'Look at Definition 10:

A 'competitor' is a player in a competition. A 'fellow-competitor' is any player with whom the competitor plays.

'Do you see the implications of that? In other words if, unless everybody has scratched except one, in which case there would be no competition, each competitor is also a fellow-competitor *and all fellow-competitors are competitors.*'

People will be trying to get within earshot as you lead the little crowd towards the fourth green.

'Do you see that young Assistant playing his second up to the 4th green?' you say. 'Obviously a fellow-competitor.'

Having planted the seed of curiosity and even doubt in the minds of the would-be mentally exact you can continue, during a pause in play, as follows:

'And look at this,' you say. ' "Through the Green." Does it mean "Through the green" or not through?'

'Exactly,' perhaps somebody will say.

'And what about striking the ball twice?' you say. Then as if opening the book at random, read on page 56:

Striking the Ball Twice. If the player strike the ball twice when making a stroke, he shall count the stroke and add a penalty stroke, making two strokes in all.

'Well,' you say, looking round mildly. 'One can only ask what is he down in?'

Having encouraged the spectators, of whom you are now the acknowledged leader, to see weaknesses in official rulings, you can then point out gaps in the regulations, means by which the spectator can achieve a status far higher than he has realized.

'There are all sorts of little ways in which spectators can legally help. See here. *A player is not allowed to build a stance.*'

Go on to explain that there is nothing against the friendly spectator who for half-a-crown will allow the competitor to use his plastic adjustable platform for playing a ball stuck four feet up a tree.*

Perhaps the domain which belongs most clearly to the onlooker is *Rub of the Green*. A splendid chance for spectators occurs for instance 'when a ball in motion' can be 'stopped or deflected by an outside agency'. In other words, if you are standing just beyond the green, and a pitch to the green is obviously going to over-run, *for you it is the decision* whether

(*a*) To stand still so that the ball can be stopped by your instep,

(*b*) To open legs and let ball through,

(*c*) To run five steps and cut the ball off before it reaches, as it were, the boundary,

(*d*) To kick it on down the hill to No Man's Land at the bottom.

* Spectator must place box without being asked to do so.

Any of these actions will bring you the respect due to an Outside Agency, a person who, if (as stated) a fore-caddy (referred to also 'as an outside agency') can 'be appointed by the Committee', has the status of someone appointed by the Committee.

The spectator can go even further. 'Competitor Must Not Seek Advice.' Good rule – but what is to prevent the benevolent spectator from giving a quiet word or two on his own, and receiving the grateful smiles thereby of many an old experienced competitor winner who has yet obviously been longing to ask a question?* Again a 'referee' is a 'person who has been appointed by the Committee to accompany players to

---

* For the spectator, the perfection of one-upness is to be observed in conversation with an important competitor while he is walking to his ball. But extraordinary dangers lurk unless one is certain of one's man. I once only extricated myself by the skin of my teeth from a situation which threatened to go badly wrong. I had been watching A. D. 'Bobby' Locke win the British Open at Lytham. A mutual friend had introduced us, and Mr Locke had very generously included me in his invitation to the celebration dinner party. Next year I was watching the first round of the Daks tournament on the East Course at Wentworth. I knew Bobby Locke was there, and not doing too well in this round. Suddenly walking down to the 7th green with the crowd, there he was, a few yards from me. Aware that Opelforth and Binks might be watching I thought I would approach him with, perhaps, a word of hopeful sympathy.

'Well, not quite Lytham, is it?' I started. I thought this would remind him of our happy meeting. To my alarm his face revealed no sign of recognition. Instead, he stopped dead in his tracks and motioned me on. I parried with what some have called a clever stroke. Without a moment's pause I continued speaking, but as if to some man *just beyond him*. An atmosphere of mystery was created. For an instant a question mark hovered, then the whole incident was dismissed. I saw Opelforth stare at me narrowly for a moment; but he made no comment.

decide questions of fact'. Fine, but how if the Referee is in fact in the Secretary's room in the club-house, sipping his third rum and orange? Does this mean that no spectator is allowed to make any remarks about any facts whatever? Quite the reverse, surely, especially if you have already established your position as Outside Agency.

I myself have made good use of one of the most decent things the Rules of Golf have ever said anywhere about spectators. Read these words:

'A person outside the match may point out the location of a ball for which search is being made.'

This person does not have to be appointed by the Committee. He could appoint himself ball-pointer-out. Let him accept his responsibilities. After a drive, he would stand in the rough, pointing at the ball. Equally, and better still, he can stand in the middle of the fairway. He can stand on the green, so long as he is pointing at the ball. In other words, in the respected position of official, he can have a ring-side position for the whole match, if he sticks at his pointing. Ideally, of course, he should wear some badge, as I do. We wore it at my prep-school. It was for being able to swim two lengths of the baths.

These suggestions only hint the beginning of the breakthrough for spectators which I am leading. The possibilities are enormous. I am at present experimenting with the official definition of partner – 'a player associated with another player on the same side'. For surely I am a player myself, and if I say 'Best of luck, Mr Gregson,' does not that constitute an association, even if he has no idea who I am? 'I was Malcolm Gregson's partner in that tournament.' Does that ring true or false? If they cry 'false' then that is the burden and the danger of the pioneer. It does not halt one's march to one's goal.

Note. Remember that the status of spectators has been *potentially* raised by the televising of Top Golf. The question is, how to get on camera. Make patient use of all those chances, described above, of seeming to be inside the barriers which keep out the crowd. For colour TV wear an easily recognizable garment. Field glasses will make people say 'he's somebody'. To gain maximum marks, seem to be talking to famous golf-watcher – Eisenhower would be perfection. Lowest marks goes to the anti-ploy of waving at the camera. Our man Cosmo sometimes makes a hit, however, by holding up a baby – somebody else's, of course.

ANIMALS AND THE SPECTATOR DOG

Dogs are not spectators in the accepted usage of this word. But there is no harm in referring to them here, even if what we are really talking about is the dog as accessory spectator or potential distraction unit.

Gamesmen and lifemen alike treat all animals with kindness and nicechap humour; and this can be a factor in golf gamesmanship. For instance, I was once driving that sound animal lifeman Willoughby to a course near Goodwood when he suddenly interrupted me.

'Better stop,' he said.

He pointed to a couple out hacking. They were approaching us at a slow trot.

'Why?' I said, accelerating to 25. The group was still 350 yards away.

'Well – rather a nice thing to do,' said Willoughby. 'You must realize that your car is a monster fearful and strange to that horse.'

'Sounds as if that horse was a pretty strange animal to *you*,' I said, rather miffed, and convinced at that moment that I had lived half my life in a stable.

'He's quite right, you know,' said Cosmo, sitting in the back of the car – bad case of M.S.U.F.*

'Of *course* he's right,' I said, with irritation, meaningless though excusable because I knew the Willoughby ploy so well. Suddenly, when helping me to look for my ball, he would take exaggeratedly long steps so as to 'be careful not to tread on them'. On what? Then there were his moments on certain holes at Westward Ho! When the sheep were on the fairways Willoughby would waste endless time to 'make

---

* Maddening Support for the Utterly Fatuous.

sure he didn't hit them'. This was especially irritating because when he did hit even a young lamb, with one of his flaccid little iron shots, it showed no reaction whatever.

'Boo!' Willoughby would shout kindly. 'Come along, Topsy!'

Women in the party at once took to him, and liked it even when he held up a pitch shot because a starling was standing on the green.

Afterwards, in the bar, Willoughby would stick to his animal loving by almost kneeling to talk to a thin-haired little peke whose only response was to growl quietly, on a steady note. Of all animals, dogs have the highest golf influence potential. That is why some Clubs, like Royal Mid-Surrey, ban their presence within the club boundaries.*

Golf course freedom for dogs increases as we go higher North. ('The higher the latitude,' said Cosmo, with one of his crushing puns.)

Nevertheless even only a slight atmosphere of 'don'ts' for dogs increases their potential. I myself have never gone further than bringing our bitch Sophy, for a few holes. The point here is that she is a small town-bred pug and is yet capable, on release, of a surprisingly high number of micturitions. 'Widdle betting' is in its infancy, but I know it is safe to wager she will

---

* No need to mention this to dog loving guest, especially Willoughby, who drives to the club with an expensive Jack Daniel. But training, cost and breeding of dog make no difference to the secretary of R.M.S. 'I'm very sorry,' he will begin; and the fact that Willoughby has had to lock his ambitious animal inside the car for three hours is a neat way not only of overcoming his Expensive Dog ploy but of reversing the process and placing him in charge, practically, of a Lost and Strayed.

top 32 before 3 holes have been played; so that your Opponent may have lost a bet before the game has got properly under way.

There is a leader in every profession and I would like to cite 'Rose', the golden labrador of 'Meaty' Bennett, as first in the art of golf course distraction. Meaty is proud of her behaviour. When he says 'Sit' Rose will sit, put on a loose-lipped openhearted smile and swish her muscular tail. When he is driving, she will take up this position automatically, sitting behind his back *on the same side of the tee as the tee box*.

The point is that Bennett was left-handed and when I came to drive myself, Bennett's months of dog training paid off. Rose was smiling at me full in the face.

Rose was quite a well behaved bitch but she had one marked characteristic: she was physically attractive to dogs. Why not? But why was she, alone among bitches, able to 'switch on', it seemed, at will, and always on the golf course? Every spacious garden around the course at Wentworth contains at least one dog, and as Rose proceeded, barricaded fences would be pounded to breaking point, and the barking would be picked up from glade to glade behind the rhododendrons.

'It doesn't put you off, does it?' shouted Meaty. But the newcomer was stunned. 'Sit' commanded Bennett just before he played his shot. Bennett did well with Rose until one day she suddenly cut across the course 80 yards in front of him and caught one of his topped two irons in her ribs. She whimpered a bit.

'Don't let this put you off,' we all said, in unison.

Dogs who move only when the owner's opponent is about to play pass hands for quite large sums. To train a dog to do this would be ungamesmanlike: but if a dog has this instinct how can one stop it? I immediately think here of Miss P. Hancock's 'Miles', who, as opponent is lining up to hit the ball, rises softly and walks across the tee, so gently, so humbly to his mistress just as her opponent is lifting his club. It is this very self-effacing quality which makes opponent feel angry and ashamed of himself at the same time.

II

SOME NOTES ON TOP GOLF

GOOD PLAY AND GOOD PLAYMANSHIP

'To call this chapter "Notes" is a ploy,' said Gattling, who was looking over my shoulder, hoping that his name would be mentioned even more often than it is.

'Suggests modesty?' I said. I quite like Gattling, but keeping his name in the background has been one of the major cares of my literary life.

'No,' said Gattling, talking a shade louder than usual. 'It suggests that you know so little about the subject that you dare not claim to be stating a principle, much less composing a definitive chapter.'

Gattling had obviously been practising this sentence before he came into the room.

'The English professional,' he went on, while I bent over the print. I loathe being interrupted when I am correcting galleys, and I knew we were going to get glimpse-of-the-obvious number 14b.

'The British pro, the American pro, is the best mannered, the hardest working ...' (and so on to the inevitable finish) ... 'and he's usually more completely a gentleman than any other person in the Club.'

'I'm sure it's true of your Club,' I said, reflecting that Gattling was the only one of my friends who used the word 'gentleman' and that he used it rather often.

To start again. One must distinguish between Top

Play and what could be called Top Playmanship. The play of golf is not the subject of this manual. The question remains, is there a basic golf leader gambit?

I have suggested some useful *individual* gambits in the second chapter. The downright toughness of J. H. Taylor, dressed perfectly for the part. The 'perfect swing' style of Vardon, contrasted with the Primitive Man persona of the much longer hitting Archie Comston or Ted Ray. But so far as a general top gambit is concerned, I would describe it as an instinctive tendency to over exemplify the practically inimitable.

Let me explain what I mean. In my Club most members want to be local top. It is not surprising, therefore, that instead of trying to learn from other local tops, they want to imitate national and international tops.

When the visiting star plays his exhibition round, they follow him with worshipful obedience, silent as mice. They will travel vast distances to starve at Sandwich, wedge into the bottle necks of Wentworth or be carved to pieces by the wind at Carnoustie. Even while watching golf on TV, they rarely talk above a whisper. And what do they learn about play? As an ardent Big Golf Watcher myself, I can give the answer.

A series of impossible, if not dangerous, examples. What do the followers of Arnold Palmer see? A fine man? Of course. But a man hitting the ball as hard as he can and saying so. Fatal model for our Wiffley, because the harder he hits the more certain he is to hit the ground three or four inches behind the ball. I suggested to Wiffley that he should imitate a different TV hero altogether, Julius Boros, who looks as if he were carelessly flicking his drive only 50 yards exactly.

It was the splendid full swing of Nicklaus which

started Gelper's trouble with his intervertebral spaces. Some golfers, including Max Faulkner of Britain and Doug Sanders of America, lead the way by winning competitions while dressed in striking clothes and un-inhibited colours. Here again imitation is dangerous. For a year or two, Gattling tried wearing sky-blue plus 2s, like Faulkner. It simply demonstrated, with painful clarity, not how like Faulkner's were his clothes but how unlike Faulkner's was his swing. I have corre-sponded by cablegram with Alistair Cooke on this problem and he tells me that

'in America, since the blooming of Doug Sanders into puce shoes and magnolia trousers any small eccentricity of color in the opponent's dress can be chucklingly, and incessantly, referred to along the way as "a touch of Sanders", always to be capped by some such addition as – "watch out for that short, stubby backswing". You then lunge into the brow-knitted very serious discussion of "How *does* he do it, with that stiff, short back swing? Maybe your arc is much longer than it seems. Anyway there's something about your game today which brings him back vividly." '

Then take Harley Chubb. In 1967 he read Gary Player's autobiography and went into strict training including finger-tip press-ups, starting with one and going on to two. For three weeks he was in a state of strict diet and training until the headaches began to come on. A year later Seligmann, in a sort of personal dedication to the achievement and hard work of Jack-lin, disappeared every evening after dark and was dis-covered in a flurry of farmyard noises practising against a driving net in his hen house. The long series of defeats which followed caused him to switch models, at the time of the Masters tragedy, to de Vicenzo. But ease, charm and the sporting spirit were not quite Seligmann either.

BE YOUR OWN CHARACTER

Here, in yet another context, appears the old Life-manship rule, 'Decide on your character and stick to it.' Top Golfer is a public figure. Whether local or national, he must realize that the only way to be remembered is (*a*) to be a little bit different, even eccentric, (*b*) never to vary and (*c*) to be easily recognizable physically as well as psychologically.

A moment's thought will show the importance, for a start, of (*c*). Where would A. D. Locke be without his white shoes, or Snead without his straw hat? If Coles smoothed his hair, or if Henry Cotton allowed his to wander, they would lose half their followers at a clap. When Palmer tucked his shirt in and gave up chain-smoking, people began to say 'Who's Palmer?' Some strong golfers, whose faces are impossible to remember from one minute to the next, do well by wearing pink trousers with violet shoes in the morning, and reversing the colours in the afternoon.

Let us summarize the types of Top Golfer. Beginners who want to stand any chance at all must choose early. 'He practised putting in his play pen,' as they always say. Intelligent readers will agree with me that an early choice of golf personality is far more important.

a) *The Dedicated.* Three up at lunch in a 36-hole match, he goes straight to the bar, makes room for himself in order to ask for soda water, then spends the lunch hour practising chips. After the match, as dusk

begins to gather, who is that lone figure marching towards the practice course? No need to say.

b) *The Part-Time.* Said to play golf only for fun. Has
several jobs, and is outstandingly good at another
game, which he plays with more passion.

c) *The 'I Say, What Shoulders!'* This type is limited
because it is limited to the gigantically strong, though I
have seen this personality pluckily assumed by two
players who were in fact only gigantically fat. Whatever he does must be done in a muscular way and *look*
strong, whatever the facts. There is a lightness in his
walk. The crowd of spectators melts momentarily, then
closes again as he passes through them on to the green.
How upright his carriage, planting his proud feet i' the
receiving turf. (Maximum waist measurement for this
type 36".)

d) *'It's Agony.'* Everything is hell. His brow is criss-
crossed by lines of suffering. The ball is in the middle
of the fairway, but (obviously from his behaviour)
the lie is just the most unfortunate in the world. He
looks at it from ground level. Shall he summon the
Referee for a ruling? No. One doesn't want to cause
trouble. Better to take it out on everybody's nerves
by walking half-way to the green to see the shot backwards. He will fling grass in the air, discuss club
with caddie, pick out his stance as if the ground was
ankle deep in broken glass, change his mind twice and
smile as if he sees the humorous side.

e) *Nothing To It.* Rather like b, but the opposite of
d, this type always has a welcome when he steps on to
the green. Rarely the winner in a competition, he yet is
seldom lower than fifth. He looks ordinary, strolls at an
ordinary pace, never has more than one practice round,

if that, and when he hits the ball, the whole thing is as perfunctory as knocking the head off a dandelion.

All five of these types have a proved audience pull, a built-in one-upness, a 'crowd-is-with-me' power, which is difficult to counter. But to gamesmanship, nothing is impossible. Alfred Stop was, of all the decent players who have never been heard of perhaps the most promising, and the one who most regularly reached the quarter finals of the Southern section of the Oxfordshire County Championship. Year after year, he found himself being balked by the crowd following some other player, such as popular Jack Rendall of Nettlebed,* who was a member of romantic Huntercombe and belonged to the Siegfried variant of the 'What Shoulders!' type.

Dotted lines represent Alfred Stop

We thought we could help Stop, and made a suggestion to him. Next year, sure enough, nobody took the slightest notice of Stop in the first two rounds, and since the competition was actually played at Huntercombe, his toes were trampled on more than ever by a particularly large number of Rendall fans. In the third round, Rendall and Stop had to meet.

* Nettlebed, pop. 758, church Perp. Without an old market cross, Nettlebed is best known as the residence of Lt Colonel Wilson, illustrator of these manuals. A stopping place for Guided Tours, his hill-top cottage, 1830, is a friendly landmark.

'My, you're popular,' said Stop, acting on our advice.

'Oh, I don't know,' said Rendall, looking round at his followers – about 25.

'Doesn't it make you nervous?'

'A-ha,' Rendall said, ambiguously. 'How do you mean?'

'Well, all those Nettlebeders, wanting you to win *for Nettlebed*.'

'Yes?'

'Peter Allis, always tremendously popular, used to say that it was his English friends *willing* him to win, which put him off –'

'I can see that,' Rendall said. He was getting cagey.

'The weight of Europe behind him. . . .'

In the end Rendall's rhythm became dislocated and Stop won. He has often returned to us for further advice; and at Christmas he sends us two of sherry and one of port. It is not our practice to accept fees.

12

WOMEN AND CHILDREN LAST

(These notes are completely expurgated.)

THE THIN END

NOT far from the ancient town of Rye there is a sea coast course famous for its mixture of rough beauty and of golf problems – problems so difficult that few men have been able to persuade themselves that women should be allowed even to set foot on it.

*'If only women would realize that they
simply must never wear trousers.'*

Nevertheless women have played this course and round about 1950 Mrs Bassett, a wife well-known in gamesmanship circles, was actually made a life member of the Club by her father, a former chairman of committee. She was entitled to play over the course and, though entry to the club-house was not allowed, she was permitted, owing to the distinguished record of her parent, to be handed drinks through a small window in a corner of the windward side.

In spite of that, this woman, Mrs Bassett, although there was a *sheltered* outdoor seat for her, used to complain openly, in January and February, and again and again older members asked themselves: how was she elected?

On one occasion she knocked on the window 'because she wanted another', and although I knew I would be criticized, I myself handed her one.

Was I wrong? Twelve years later a woman's room was built. It had a dainty little shelf and a sort of cupboard door which, when opened, led to the back of the bar. But long before that happened I myself took Mrs Bassett to the Woking Club. I was not disappointed. There there was a small women's changing room, complete with wash-basin and a coat-hanger which (she told me with shining eyes) 'although it had the name Mrs Wilson on it was regarded as being free for use when Mrs Wilson was not present'. But what she did not at first realize was that provided she stuck to a pre-arranged route, clearly recognized and agreed upon, she could walk, partly *through the club premises*, to a dining room *where men and women ate together*. I remember her coming in now, hiding so perfectly her excitement.

Now women are only on a one-to-four inferiority in the club-house. And I think one can call it a happy outcome that as a result of this the atmosphere of golf gamesmanship, in clubs, has thickened. 'All women are natural lifewomen' – and, therefore, basically gameswomen.

MAN *v.* WOMAN

Let us take that fine gamesmanship encounter, the singles match man *versus* woman. The woman will know the basic ploys, but her version may not be immediately recognized by the man for what it is. If he is a kind of C. E. Rimming type, who wants to get on, keep going, believes somebody must be the organizer, especially with women present, he will feel sure he is going to be held up. The woman can whip up this tension by creating little delays. To start with, just before they go to the first tee, she can suddenly disappear. 'To be expected?' thinks Rimming, and buys two re-paints. New equipment impresses the ladies, he believes. But where is she? This is impossible. The first tee happens to be beautifully empty. The delay is intolerable. In a moment he is standing on forbidden ground, outside the women's changing room.

'Mrs Bassett!' he calls in a strange muted voice. 'H.' – a shouted whisper, for he dislikes Christian names. And then he hears through the door *her* voice – *in laughing conversation*.

Calmer men than Rimming will find this hard to bear. Pipchild had a splendid way of getting women out. 'You're wanted on the telephone,' he would sing in a silky voice. 'Some man.' When she does appear at last, perhaps, annoyingly, just in time to drive off, she will not have been allowed to tie to her trolley some small long-haired dog. By way of revenge she may be carrying an immense handbag, balanced on the handle of the trolley in such a way that the bottom of the golf bag rubs and trails along the ground, and the whole trolley, if the slope of the land is over 30 degrees, will fall slowly over sideways.

MIXED FOURSOMES

If Mrs King-Porter was my partner in a foursome against the Rimmings, I can say that nine times out of ten we would win. In later life Rimming's phobia about holding people up got worse. Last year he actually took me into his confidence about this. It was at the time of our Autumn Meeting and Rimming was out of it. He had pneumonia but the antibiotic brigade gave the pneumonia no chance. I went along to tell Rimming all about my morning's golf.

'I managed to pip Scatter by one stroke,' I said.

'Amazing,' he said. 'Didn't you go mad – with his fiddling about, I mean?' said Rimming.

'Oh, I don't know,' I said, in a warmer kinder voice. 'That's *him*, isn't it?'

'My God, it's not me,' said Rimming, as the Nurse came to take his temperature. 'Do you know that once, at Muirfield, when the captain had especially arranged a foursome for us, the captain was playing behind us *and asked to come through*? I could have sunk through the earth.'

Rimming was sweating slightly, and after the nurse had read the thermometer, when she was shaking it down she put on that frighteningly expressionless look which, to me, means 102 degrees as a minimum. I doubt if the Muirfield incident really happened: but when the Rimmings were drawn against us in the Spring Mixed foursomes Mrs King-Porter played up splendidly. If it were her drive she took a minute getting off the tee. On the fifth green the two young men behind were walking slowly up to play their seconds.

'Shall we let them through?' said Rimming, who knew that one of the players was a guest wearing super golf shoes – an obvious 6 or under.

'If we do we'll have to let five other lots through as well,' said K-P, taking out a very small pocket mirror and staring at a lower eyelash.

'Do if you like,' she went on. She had a discouraging way of not talking to the person she was talking to.

Another thing Kingers did even I found quite deeply distracting. Rimming and I were pretty silent in this foursome because we knew our concentration would be taxed to the uttermost. But Kingers, as if to show how superior women were as a *social* animal, and what fun they had in life generally, would during the match start four new subjects of conversation with Mrs Rimming with such bubbling enthusiasm that I must admit that I have slipped unobtrusively behind them to find what it was about; but somehow the words bounce off one's brain, and I forget them instantly.

Last time we were dormy 2 up on the Rimmings and at that very moment, on the tee together before they drove, they simultaneously realized that Esmeralda Quick was in England and 'was almost unrecognizable'. Mrs Rimming topped her drive of course and so did King-Porter: but the effect on Rimming was final. Even if he had laid his impossible second dead no one would really be watching. The women would keep silent on the stroke for the regulation half minute but nobody would really appreciate it. Even I was edging over a little to get news of Esmeralda. Unrecognizable from *what*?

SPLIT PLAY

I have written elsewhere of the possibility, in the Mixed, of sowing the seed of mistrust between the partners of the opposing side. *Man* should be extra attentive to opposing *woman*, helping her over style,

giving a brief tug to her trolley every now and then, saying 'good shot' when she has just missed a putt, twisting his head full towards her when she is speaking to him, to suggest attentiveness, even a strange feeling of attraction.

Object of this: to induce feeling 'Why doesn't *my*

partner behave likewise?' This has some real chance against certain husband and wife partnerships especially one in which the husband, although he knows he shouldn't, can't keep silent any longer and raps out a word of advice. '*No – no*, darling.'

(For 'darling' in this context read 'non-darling'.)

'*No – not* straight for the flag.'

Wife may want revenge more than victory, and may miss ball altogether.*

YOUNG PERSONS

Older persons must take special care when playing with young people aged between 14 and 18. This group tends to think itself above the law in such matters as clothes, or never thinks of them, and above all never wears anything suitable, preferring for instance thin pointed suede shoes for wet grass, gumboots

on a sunny day, and a tight roll-top sweater to make swinging difficult.

Julian Judd and Millicent Priors developed our 'in love' gambit, which had some success. Both were sound players: but under favourable conditions, with one watching the other play, or teaming up in a foursome, they were able to pretend that it wasn't the game they

* See Oman, C., *History of Warfare in the Middle Aged*, p. 408.

were interested in; they had only eyes for each other. Opponents, smiling paternally would take it easy and then, suddenly, in the last 5 holes, the Judd–Priors combination would start to play grimly with full concentration and a look-out for any slackness in the rules by their opponent. If playing for money, they sat down after the game was over and divided their winnings equally. To me, once or twice a loser in such matches, there was something chilling about this. At the same time Jay and young Charlie, of our Club, really were in love. We all tried extra hard not to let the chance of youthful good looks, and the fact that they were inclined to hold hands, take the edge off our determination to win against them. Some, however, were flustered by the impression they gave – by clever gamesmanship we realized – that they did not mind losing.

CHILD CARE

All gamesmen love children, and that is exactly why they must be especially on their guard with the child golfer. Allow them to carry your bag and even give them a graduated scale of payment (penny a hole is the least which, currently, will be accepted). But when the child begins to play, be careful to stop those *full, careless swings*, which may occasionally, by that thousand to one chance, send their ball farther than your own. Forbid them to run after the ball, and there must be no jumping across bunkers – which anybody can do in gym shoes. In general let them not act as if games were play.

The darker side of child golfing is shown in a tendency not to stick to the rules. Children *must be pre-*

vented from teeing up their ball on a sandcastle if they go in a bunker. And why, in this well-known picture is Agnes, his mother, standing so close to the infant Odoreida? To make sure he does not improve his lie, have no doubt of it.

13

SCHOOL OF ADVANCED STUDIES

THE student who has read and revised the foregoing chapters may now call himself something of a golf gamesman. He will be familiar with the principle ploys. He will be able to reply to them with the appropriate counters.

Nor will he neglect, I hope, to incorporate in his play gambits first devised for another game altogether. I once watched a match between a Frenchman, Etienne Tortelier, and a thorough-going Englishman of the grouchy school. I soon realized that M. Tortelier, said to be a cousin of the brilliant interpreter of the Walton cello concerto, had only read *Gamesmanship*, and this only in the shortened version published in France. *Yet he was adapting, for golf, a technique recommended by me for the snooker table*. Etienne was quick, responsive, appreciative, sympathetic. Bi-lingual from the age of eight, he now brilliantly reverted, when in Britain, to a slightly unidiomatic halting English which charmed everybody except his opponent.

'Rather in luck with the bounceeng,' he would say, having quite correctly played to induce a pull on his drive to the long 14th. A hole or two later, Mott the Magnificent Male, Mott the Monosyllabic, his opponent, landed his ball behind a newly planted sapling. Tortelier was in a little agony of regrets.

'Your gardener wants to make a new landscape then? That tree sprang from the nothing?'

At the next hole Tortelier's drive curved out of sight. 'Bunkair, bunkair,' he called but he knew and I knew that the ball was short of real trouble in a patch of temptingly easy semi-rough. Tortelier had read our suggestions for Bad Luck Play. And one glance at Mott

from F. Wilson's *Personalities of the Far Eastern Golf Scene*

revealed that he was one of those golfers who believed that fate was against him before he struck his first drive. At the first unlucky rub of the green, 'Here we go again,' he would say: and by no means always to himself.*

GAMBITS FOR SPECIAL OCCASIONS

Adapt – borrow – improvise. That is what we expect from the qualified golf gamesman. A simple act, a

* I am reminded of old 'Gravy' Penrose who died in 1928 at the age of 80. All through life he was pursued by the thought that things were going to go against him at golf *but through his own fault*. If I had not heard this myself, in 1927, I would not repeat the story. But I can confirm that he called out, explosively, 'Oh my God, what a fool I am' *before he'd hit the ball*, at the start of the down swing.

commonplace utterance, can if well chosen sow the seed of distraction.

SUDDEN REMARKS

For instance, what could be more innocuous than an 'I was never a *member* of the party', thrown in as you walk down the path to a couple of well-placed drives in the middle of the fairway? What 'party'? The Let's All Speak Celtic Association, or – could it be – the C.P.? Opponent can scarcely ask, but his mind returns to it, more than once.

'Are you sure that you are not naturally a left-handed player?' can produce a similar moment of un-ease: or simply 'Binkie caught a thirty-two pound carp last Sunday.' Or – if you are a member of the Com-mittee – try 'I understand we're not going to be allowed to cash cheques any more,' (looking intently at opponent). It's a question of an instinct for the man and the moment.

IS THIS 'GROUND UNDER REPAIR'?

Here is another situation which tests the enterprise of the senior gamesman. He may not mind whether it is ground under repair or not. His ball may have a per-fectly reasonable lie anyhow. But it is often helpful to make as much fuss as possible of such a situation. In competition play Ackminster, who made his own golf pegs and prided himself on his straightforwardness, was often prepared to go back to the club-house and find the referee if necessary, even if no one was sure who he was. This caused such misery that Ackminster was made a member of the Local Rules Committee, and this did cut short this particular ploy.

Ackminster believed down to the roots of his small, efficient little moustache, that everything, including the pleasures of golf, could be achieved by accuracy of wording. ' "Shall" or "will" not drive if the 8th tee is occupied?' Ackminster knew the answer.

'That makes us dormy one up, then?' said Scatters pleasantly.

'Only if you insist on stopping if we win the 18th,' said Ackminster. 'In which case it's my match.'

Later on I saw Scatters miserably at the bar, by himself.

'Cheer up,' I said. 'Leave it to me.' I suppose I'm silly but I love helping people: and in a minute or two I suggested that it *might* be possible to get 'Accuracy Ackers' on the wrong foot. Scat rose to the occasion and next time they played together he got Ackers with a good old beauty. Ackminster's ball was ten inches from the hole.

'Under the circumstances,' said Scat, 'I'll give you that putt.'

'Thanks,' said Ack., 'but how you can be *under* something which is *around*, you, *circum*, beats me, if I may say so.'

'Excuse me most frightfully,' said Ack., 'but I believe you've got the wrong sense of "under".'

'Oh yes?' said Scatter, expecting a leg-pull.

'Here it's "under" in the sense of "within" – 3rd meaning in the Big Oxford.'

Ackers lost the next 3 holes and the match, partly because of the shock of being given a putt of three feet* at the 15th, but principally because Scatters

---

* Nearing the end of the historic 36 hole blood match at St George's between John Blackwell and Alec Hill, the match was still all square at the hole before the Canal Hole – the 31st. On

seemed strangely confident. Rushing home to his dictionaries, Ackminster was faced with the truth. Verbally, his day was done. The quality of his game did not allow him to revive by actual golf.

BAD WEATHER PLAY

A sure sign of the advanced gold gamesman is that he is never caught out by rough weather. He certainly doesn't complain of it. To admit to frozen fingers is an elementary error. Wind 'makes the course more interesting'. Rain 'makes it possible for your second shot at the long 13th to stop on the green', you say, if you happen to know that on wet ground your opponent will rarely reach it in 4.

Our expert rainman is G. Paine, who always had a special 'umbrella caddy' standing by to supplement his regular one, and for a match even a third, whose sole purpose is to produce a perpetual supply of dry towels. This act of the otherwise quite popular Paine is said to irritate more people in our circle, for a larger variety of reasons, than any other ploy in our armoury.

Gamesmen will never give the impression that they are splashing about in the mud. I will not give the name of the professional who so superbly kept his dignity during the storm somewhere in the Thames Valley last Summer. He was a bad rainsman and had taken 5s to the turn. Suddenly his pale and tragic profile was seen emerging from a half-way hut. 'We've been told to

---

the green each were about $5\frac{1}{4}$ feet from the hole. After careful measuring it was judged to be Blackwell's putt. He holed and then picked up Hill's ball, giving Hill a half. Endlessly repeating to himself, 'Why did he do it?' Hill is said to have become distracted, and so lost.

come in,' he said, in his slightly doom-tinged voice. Had some kind of rocket been let off?

'Back,' somebody* echoed, in a sing-song voice.

As they all splashed towards the club-house one or two thought 'Yes'. Of course no 'unplayable weather' recall had been issued: but it was the day they were testing aircraft for the sonic boom. A coincidence? An example of that initiative and opportunism which the good gamesman must always keep ready at the hip? I prefer to think that the idea was spontaneous, and based on nothing, and that this professional, concealed in his hut, himself made a sound, less difficult than it seems, of a distant boom.

RARE PLOYS AND PECULIAR INSTANCES

Initiative. Opportunism. Is not this the true achievement of the good gamesman, nay lifeman?

Adaptability means One-upness in the evolution stakes.

I have collected here a few examples of this essential initiative – description sometimes brief, of inventiveness in the dealing with diverse yet not uncharacteristic situations.

Col. Dennison is a good golfer, member of that darkly fascinating course on which he so often beat me. But it is not of him I am speaking. Of no value to our purpose, his success has always been based on good play. No. It is the fact that this course is in Trades Union country and is played on by many Trades Unionists, anti Trades Unionists and Trades Unionists who are anti Unions or just simply against Trade. Not surpris-

* Obviously another man who had done badly, and knew that if play was stopped all scores would be cancelled.

ingly, a Unionist of a visiting team, always picked because though handicapped at 8 he was a genuine 2 and capable of playing this course in par, decided to revenge himself on his own club secretary, who had refused him free transport, by playing no better than his official handicap.

ANTI ANTI-SEMITE PLAY

May I drag myself in here by mentioning another semi-political ploy which I once used? One of the most un-Clubworthy men I ever met was O'Seamus O'Toole, a loud voiced conversation stopper who emptied club bars like magic by roaringly offering to buy people drinks in return for two seconds of their attention. I happened to know he'd been blackballed from the Golf Club of my friend Binstead, fairly well-known hurdler and Liberal candidate. We were playing Pebble Beach, or, rather, *vice versa* – it is not an easy course.

'Oh, so you've pilled O'Toole,' I said, as we waited on the 18th tee – I was four over fives, but I was one up. We were talking about his home club.

'What? Oh – well, frankly, yes,' said Binstead, who was on the Committee. 'How did you know?'

'Pity,' I said, taking no notice of this question.

'Pity?'

'Rough diamond,' I said. 'But I'm afraid he'll find it difficult to get in anywhere else.'

'I should say so.'

'Being Jewish,' I went on, after a pause of three seconds.

'*What?*' said Binstead. 'It's not *possible*. *Jewish?*'

I didn't point out that unless Galt's Law was bilge

we all of us had Jewish blood. I just let it simmer. The eighteenth, at Pebble Beach, is straight but by no means easy. No need to say 'I expect they get a lot of that sort of thing out here too.' I did not think that Roger would win that hole.

ONE FOR THE FIRST HOLE

There is a mystique of bar behaviour and of offering or not offering suitable or unsuitable people drinks. This question is always before us and I have often returned to it.

'But what about drink before play?' some have said to me, and here behaviour, even among accredited gamesmen, varies sharply from man to man. In terms of actual golf, the drinking of two ports or two kümmels after lunch is equivalent to 2 or $2\frac{1}{2}$ down on the afternoon round (see p. 56). But is not the suggestion of 'to hell with it' implied by such behaviour itself putting off, inclined to make more temperate opponent feel as if he himself were playing life in steel-rimmed spectacles, a slightly out-of-it player in a Society meeting? 'Buffalo' Strang was well aware of this but he had had some part of the body, believed to be the pan-

Bangkok resident to Rookie opponent: 'No need to give him anything extra.' (F. Wilson, op. cit.)

C. Tickler (15) never had a car without a built-in bar.
At his Club, the Castlemayne Country, it was car,
not golf handicap, which counted.

creas, taken clean out, and my medical knowledge told
me that without his pancreas, or something damned
like it, a large whiskey would make Strang lose sense of
distance. I was interested, therefore, to see how well
Strang had perfected the art of drinking gin and tonics
without gin, and whiskey and ginger ale without
whiskey.

Drink is a great subject for exhausting jokes, and
Cosmo Tickler, naturally, exploited this to the full. I
remember Gelper's 'expressionless' look when he saw
Cosmo T. offer a breathalyzer to Cardew, his partner,
just before starting the final of the foursome. My advice is, as always: if in doubt, be one thing or the other.
Whether or not you like to carry a flask disguised as a
hand warmer,* publicly you will drink nothing but
milk, and be clear and exact in manner on the first tee
after lunch.

* Like Ackminster. The heat holes in the surface were, of
course, imitation.

The obvious danger here is that Clear-Eye may send the ball 10 yards into the rough. So say the chief practitioners of the rival group. The alternative method entails slipping in for a stiff-looking settler at 9.30 a.m. before starting; making an unobtrusive dash to the club-house if any of the middle holes pass close, and, during the lunch break drinking or seeming to drink just one more whiskey or kümmel than anybody else. The advantage here is, obviously, that if you slice your first afternoon drive into the woods you can just say 'Gone with the wind' and everybody will rather like you. And if – and this is the ideal – you hit the ball, straight and long, opponents will think 'One must take one's hat off to old Sloshpot,' will wonder if they're not missing something and will be suddenly very much less sure about winning the match.*

* I do think Odoreida's variant on this ploy is worth mentioning. He too made one dash for the club-house during the match. When he returned he would 'accidentally' allow a *syringe* to drop from his pocket, which he would hurriedly retrieve. Even Seligmann's concentration was affected on one occasion. He lost two holes – and two more when he found, to his anger, that the 'syringe' was really a fountain pen filler.

In other words, 'be one thing or the other' – though I am not at all sure that Julius Strelto, who often joined our party when he was over from the States, did not overdo it all with the portable bar specially built into his golf bag, with special compartments for lemon slicer and a side flap for the vegetable parts of a Pimms No. 1.

LIFE PEOPLE PLAY

That remarkable book *Games People Play* has been said to be the only readable, if not indeed also the best work on the psychology of behaviour never to have actually come from our own research H.Q. at Yeovil. Dr Berne, the author, shows us that when the father, sitting up late, reprimands his daughter for coming home at 2 a.m., and there is a row ending in a general banging of doors, the whole thing is a pattern of tribal beliefs, a sort of ritual war dance of the kind still mimicked by the Pueblo Indians of Santa Fe. The reality behind the row may be the father's jealousy of the young, his dislike of strangers or the fact that his wife, the evening before last, amusingly scored off him at a bridge party.

I myself have always said that when Wren seemed to be trying to please us with St Paul's he was really getting his own back on Baines, the King's builder, who said that large domes could never be supported without adventitious under-pinning. And (I have often asked) when Einstein first formulated Relativity, what relative had he in mind?

How does this affect the golfman? He will see at once that when he is playing golf he is not playing golf – a truism that all gamesmen should bear in mind.

'Gee, you really hit that one,' says Pitt's opponent Poke. Indeed Poke is a little uneasy because he feels somewhere below the mental level that Pitt hit that drive so hard because the golf ball had suddenly changed into an image of Poke's own head, and that he was being decapitated from a peg tee, Poke having just

got a job in the office which Pitt had fancied might be, must be, coming his way. Meanwhile Poke's shorter drive was in the rough. Feeling a mysterious tingling sensation on the back of his neck, he yet played out sensibly not for the hole but for the centre of the fairway, knowing that by steadiness and dependability he could become Deputy Director of Clay Imports Subsidiaries.

The golf gamesman can make use of these facts. Saxe, a bit of a psycho himself, was good at it. Sometimes Boyce's five-foot putt would stop just short of the hole. It was a fault of his.

' "Willing to wound and yet afraid to strike",' the old quotesman would say, and it was annoying because there was something in it – a theory I would like to present to Dr Berne for his comments.

Or one can go back to classical psycho-analytic theory, to Freud, particularly on the putting green. And if a man is a fluffer of short chips, you can rub it in by telling him that 'there's an excellent little man in Curzon Street – a perfectly O.K. address for doctors nowadays. He's changed his name from Leslie to Lazlo. Marvellous little man. Gets you to talk to him under sedation. Gets you right in less than three months.'

GARY PLAYER'S FATHER

I see from his autobiography that Gary Player is grateful for the fact that his father was a landscape gardener. He suggests that this is an advantage because having landscape gardening in the blood, so to speak, increases his quickness in getting the lie of the land. It makes it more easy for him to grasp contours and hidden slopes, I expect he says to an opponent faced with an early start, still a little swimmy, and off line with his putts.

(Friends of Joe Davis, the greatest snooker player in history, were anxious to introduce him to golf. At first he was a spectator only. His critical gaze was steady, even a little cold. 'Why do they hit the ball up to the hole when they want to hit it in?' he said.)

Good stuff – but it was no use Tickler claiming the same sort of advantage as Player 'because his father was an estate agent'.

'It gives me a sense of boundaries,' he said. Maybe, but it didn't stop him slicing out of the course at the Canal Hole every single time he was allowed to play at Royal St George's. It is important not to boast of one's father's profession where no real advantage exists.

'My father is an astronomer,' said Toffman, and got no reply.

'It gives me a sense of distance,' he went on, looking round rather *smirkingly*, I fancied.

'I thought telescopes were supposed to reduce distance,' said Scatter pleasantly, so relaxed that his mouth was half open. But Toffman was a guest on our course.

'How far to the flag?' he asked Cosmo. I knew at once we were in for a string of bad jokes.

'About five light years,' Cosmo started. So it went on.

JOAD'S 'PLOY OF EMANCIPATION'

C. E. M. Joad was a philosopher, a fine teacher, a good games player, the best of the celebrated original Brains Trusters and, I am proud to say, my friend. He also was three times holder of the Unconscious Gamesmanship Championship. Some of his breath-taking exploits, before the war, I have already described in *Gamesmanship* where his classic lawn tennis ploy ('kindly say clearly please whether the ball is in or out') has been described at enormous length.

Some of Joad's golf ploys have also been mentioned – particularly his Indifference to Presence of Secretary play before nervous young opponent. Then there was his attempt to go to the Berkshire without actually being a member. Another – original, simple, never before described – can conveniently be regarded here.

In the summer Cyril Joad and I used to go down to the New Forest. We stayed in the charming little pub at Brook and played golf there. The idyllic nature of this Brook course delighted Joad, who was a great nature man in a sort of early left wing or Fabian style. Before he chose any country spot, he would search the skyline. One sight of a big chimney or pylon, however distant, and Cyril would pack up his bags and write a letter to the *News Chronicle*.

But Brook was perfection; and as Cyril walked through the bracken to the first tee, his way of breathing the air made me feel healthy, too.

Joad played more briskly than usual and we kept our place easily among the week-end players. Many of the holes run down to the little stream along the boundary; but surprisingly, so far, we hadn't touched water.

'Doesn't it tempt you?' said Joad.

'Not in the least,' I said, with a sudden wild suspicion. But Joad hadn't trained himself to be Top Emancipator for nothing.

'It won't take long,' he said. After some struggles with braces and the unlacing of boots, Joad was suddenly standing nude on the edge of the water, a fine figure. I could not forbear looking back. Already the mixed foursome behind was within range and seemed to have stopped uncertainly.

'Feeling shy?' Joad called as he leapt in. Impossible to shout 'not exactly'.

'Shall I let these people through?' I called.

'Yes – yes,' said Cyril largely, shutting his eyes as if to blot out everything but the feel of nature, rippling coldly round his calves.

'How about the next lot?' I said, because Major Lockyer of Beaulieu was close behind.

'Let them pass if they want to,' Joad said in his driest, most crackling Bertrand Russell voice. It was like a sort of dream because no one seemed to comment on Joad, or even notice him. It was I who felt nervy, and my game suffered too, because of the maddening way Joad assumed that I was *shocked by nudity*.

'You see? The human body isn't such a terrible thing, is it?'

I couldn't say No and I couldn't say Yes. If the gamesmanship is completely unconscious I'm done.

Result. Potter lost 3 and 2.

ADVANCED GAME LEG PLAY: THE PROBLEM OF G. PAINE

I had the privilege of observing game leg play in its purest form when I first met G. Paine at Littlestone in August 1962. I had often admired him from afar at Woking and I had encountered a vaguely similar situation in the same area soon after the war. P. Dickinson, of Rye, used to let me play against him on this course. I knew he had been a Cambridge blue and it was pleasing to me to end up not far behind him in our match. Occasionally I won.

I did not know that in the last year of the war he had broken his back, serving with the Eighth Army. I only knew that his movements seemed restricted. Occasionally I would refer to the fact that I'd 'beaten a Cambridge blue'. In a year or two he had partly recovered, and I never got near to winning again. The fun of our contests rather went out of it, for me.

A few years later the possibility of genuine game leg play, always latent as we grow older, became a reality for me. As a result not actually of a war wound but a fall in a picture gallery, I developed osteo-arthritis of the right hip. At first my golf was extremely restricted but it settled down and I was able to play normally except that my game, never very long, was now decidedly short.

Needless to say I brought my leg in as much as possible. I was once a huge hitter, people were led to believe, but now a weak hip undermined the full thrust of the right leg.

It was just at that moment that I met a golfer who had no right leg whatever, and no right hip joint either. The whole thing had been shot away in the last engagement beyond the Rhine, in the last week of the war.

The link between Geoff Paine and myself was that he was 'interested in Gamesmanship'. What exactly did this mean? Anyhow I was pleased to give him a game. He used crutches, but before playing the shot handed them to his remarkably pretty wife or to his caddy and then played his shot *balancing on one leg*. This I was not prepared for. Mustn't beat him too easily, I thought. On the first tee he took a rhythmical swing as he balanced. Then. *Pifff*. What had happened? His ball, 225 yards away, was remarkably near the first green.

Of course if I'd ever been in that rank of golf I should have known all about it. G. Paine had been Scratch at the age of 16, and plus 2 at 18, just before the War. On leave he had had astounding success against all our leading players. He still had enormous strength. On one leg, he was still able to go round in 75.

Here, surely, was the one-up position to beat all one-up positions. What was the good of my slowing up about the 12th hole and complaining of pain in the right hip if G. had no right hip to have a pain in? I only know that, against Paine, however many strokes I received, I always lost.

One must admit that Paine makes brilliant use of his handicap. To take one example, if he chips his ball up three feet from the hole, he will stand his ground, be silent and make no further movement. He seems suddenly to be looking particularly tired. 'Thank goodness I won't, surely, be asked to putt *that*,' he seems to be saying to himself. And even though one understands every move of that particular gambit, just try

Surely he won't ask me to putt that one?

asking him to make the stroke. The laborious start towards the middle of the green. His caddy (an old friend) particularly solicitous. The manipulation of the crutches half fumbled, from fatigue. It is the glance from the caddy which I find most difficult to bear.

Paine has beaten us at ping-pong, using only one crutch. Needless to say we didn't at first send him short ones. Quite soon we were trying to do short ones all the time. But it was no good. It is only at croquet and snooker that we can still hold him. Our last snooker game was, frankly, a nightmare.

I have sent this problem round to all our leading gamesmen. T. Rattigan, our No. 4, posted me a characteristic communication, but it is of doubtful value. Here is a typical extract (Subject: the Problem of Paine):

If you funk having your own leg amputated I would suggest turning up on the first tee walking on your knees with *both* legs strapped behind your thighs. J. Ferrer in a film called *Moulin Rouge* about some painter chap tried the same ploy to excellent effect.

We welcome fellow suggestions from fellow gamesmen, and we welcome them when they are truly practical.

14

U.S. *VERSUS* U.K.

SOMETHING must be said in this book of the games-manship of Anglo-American golf play, U.S. *v.* U.K.* with particular reference to the U.K. man in the U.S. and occasional reflections on the American in Britain.

How stands all this today? So far as top golf is concerned, America has established a massive one-upness. We, of London, bring congratulations to American top golfers, but it does not stop us from being deeply fed up.

Here, surely, is the prime problem of International Gamesmanship. How to make the invincible vincible. How to reduce the great American one-up to parity.

HINTS FOR THE SALT OF THE EARTH

Before we put forward our first pioneering proposals for international golf, let us discuss a few basic principles, with special reference to the ordinary average or salt-of-the-earth golfer, so-called because salt is typical handicap 10.

Lifemanship's attitude to America is well-known but it should be cleared up. Where new things are con-

* My own view is, at present, definitely a minority one. But I hold increasingly to the belief that Britain and the U.S. should play on the same side, so far as golf is concerned. I envisage matches against France for instance. We and the States are brothers.

cerned, America is more-so, England less, and *vice versa* with the old, it may be said, even if there are more exceptions than there is rule.

Since the publication of *Gamesmanship* America has excelled in going one further in gamesmanship as well. Let us take one instance – the original Ploy of the Straight Left Arm (recalled here above). On the New Canaan course, in play with R. Massey, I found the technique already in use *and improved*, by this version of the essential dialogue or 'parlette':

U.S. GAMESMAN: I was going to say do you mind if I watch your drive rather close, from here? I think I know *why* you're shooting them so straight.

OPPONENT: Oh yes?

U.S. GAMESMAN: It's that spiral movement starting *from the left instep*.

What one must ask onself, when *v.* America, is 'Have they any weaknesses?' Is your U.S. friend inclined to health fads, for instance? Are some Americans allergy-minded herbalistical hypochondriacs? No harm in asking your man, anyhow, whether there is bone in his shirt buttons, or telling him that the ring you are wearing has an iodine core and you don't know what you'd do without it.

Another method, when the Americans are being more so in golf, is to try to be more more so than their more so. English golfers who reach the heart of the American golf belt sometimes write exaggerated accounts of the 'Ordeal by American Four Ball', in which 'believe it or not, every shot is played out, including the tiddliest putt'.

'What, not if it's eighteen inches?' says admiring stay-at-home.

'Yes, even if it's two inches,' says traveller, calmly. 'We started at 9.30 and came in at 4,' he goes on, laying it on slightly. 'Two rounds, you may well think. . . . Not a bit of it. One.'

'What about lunch?' says novice.

'Lunch at 4.30,' says Traveller.

'Any tea?' said Wiffley, whose Farthest West was Barnstaple.

'No.'

During my first year of playing four balls in America I made the mistake of referring nostalgically to my Wednesday morning meetings for golf with Edgar Lansbury, when we always got through two rounds by lunch time. I at once noticed that the look of admiration I had expected simply was not there, and nobody made any comment whatever. Indeed a strong article of mine, friendly but firm, which I titled 'American Golf – Speed Up!' was sent back by the *New Yorker* and the *Saturday Evening Post*.

'If prejudice against a view exists, change sides.' This has always been my rule. And this is my present policy. *Be more so than the more so.*

In other words I decided, in the four ball, to be the slowest. I held it up. A touch here, a device there. I cleaned my ball on the green – but first I unscrewed a tin and sprinkled a little shampoo powder on the wet sponge. A small 'Speedi' portable drier useful for hurrying up moisture evaporation on the ball yet took up time because the leads needed fixing to a battery inserted in the golf bag. I specialized in flattening out pitchmarks, not only on the line of my ball to the hole but beyond it.

'Why do you do that?' said one of my American opponents, with friendly curiosity, smiling.

'So often the ball deviates from the straight after passing the hole,' I said. 'We want to minimize this risk.'

'It takes time,' he said, thoughtfully.

'Half an hour a hole, Cyril reckoned, on the Downs

Course (Eastbourne),' I said. 'Why rush?' I was inventing at random of course, but I wanted to bring in C. J. Tolley, whose hand I shook in 1923.

Of course a lot can be done on both sides with national habits of hospitality, differences in changing room standards, agreements by small golf ball nations to use large ball, and *vice versa*. Talk about golf ball diameters must leave a trace of confusion, particularly if a decimal point is involved, and when expert opinion seems to state that the small ball is easier *and* that it is impossible to win if you play with it.

Americans must pride themselves on their hospitality which is kind, imaginative and refreshing, thereby putting an unfair burden on guest golf opponent, who is likely, if he tries to get the better of his noble opponent, to feel remorse – something which in its most exaggerated form can mean the loss of three straight holes.*

* Cf. losing behaviour of Valjean, potentially a 7 handicap man, in the first episode of *Les Miserables*, after stealing the bishop's candlesticks.

Odoreida, invited through some error or misprint, found himself staying in a gracious and leisurely home, near Charleston, Va. At breakfast, he did not want the beautiful bacon, crisp yet mild, and the simple perfection of egg. He wagged his foot.

'Have you any brown bread with sultanas in it?' he said. There was always a suspicion of wheeze in his voice.

'And if you've got it, Keiller's marmalade. No chance of the *Yorkshire Post*?' he added.

So far as the comforts and hospitality of American club changing-rooms are concerned, what is the English visitor to do?

A Canadian gamesman goes round taking photographs as if he were a professional – 'the Brussels edition of *Paris Match* ... interested in your *moeurs* – it means your life, the sort of people you are ... yellow filter ...' He then takes a low angle shot of some woman asleep on a balcony who, he says, 'is' this place (ugliest woman present).

THE RIGOR CUP

But we must not shirk the prime problem: the one-upness of American golf. Year after year either the professional contests, the Rigor Cup, or the Amateur, the Walkover, (to say nothing of the ever charming Courtesy Cup) turn up to remind us of the old sequence. The British captain is 'full of confidence'.* Our fine English professionals, at home and among themselves the dashing destroyers of par, the Herculean drivers, gymnasts of the iron and wizards of the green, are most

---

* Always bad gamesmanship, this non-ploy is borrowed from the world of boxing.

(but not all of them) transformed, when they get to the States or play against them here, into the kind of player who, one up and one to play, is destined, inevitably, cowed by some grim gods of the Americas, biting the hand which bit them, to take three putts.

Superstition aside, by what forces are they controlled? I will enumerate them.

(1) By the atmosphere and suggestion, artificially produced by Britain, that for Britain everything is about as serious as a major operation. This is something to do with the English Press, implacably leaden hearted on these occasions and the traditional ENGLAND FACED WITH DISASTER type of headline, which in June means that three England wickets have fallen at Lord's before lunch time.

(2) By the sense that to the American players, inevitably, it is all a gentle interlude. Where in October 1967 was Julius Boros on the day before the Ryder Cup started? Practising on the difficult Champions course? He was fishing on the bank of the water hazard.

(3) By the sense that though, for him, the British Professional, the pay is worth earning, the American players know they are probably losing money. Here we are faced with the one-upness of the preternaturally prosperous.

(4) By a sense of the inevitability of history, and the feeling that we were once so they must be now.

Here is a problem worthy of the highest gamesmanship. If I were to leave to my heirs a plan of attack, I am sure now of the general trend. Be more, or be the opposite, should be my guiding principle. As for seriousness, why not go the whole hog, spend the night before the match in meditation, and light a little fire, as a sacrifice, at break of day? Be on the practice tee at first light. Associate yourself with a peculiar religion. 'A dedicated man,' they will say.

But I would prefer places in the team to be given to the happy-go-lucky, the dashing, the debonair, and the handsome. We have not yet discussed the importance of looks in international golf. Many British players are handsome but they are not produced properly. Besides being handsome he has to look handsome. As for money let them be financially independent or perhaps real estate men with oil interests, to whom a million dollars, plus or minus, is rather small feed to men who could and would buy the golf course if they wanted to.

As for the inevitability of history, keep repeating that progress is not a series of slices piled up like a club sandwich, that regress is just as common, and that according to Spengler, and possibly Toynbee, the beacon of American golf eminence may be showing already the dubious and phosphorescent light of incipient decay. I intend, when I meet Arnold Palmer, to tell him this, in almost exactly these words.

TO EACH COURSE ITS OWN DÆMON

Daemon in Latin: δαίμων in Greek. The different spelling is a reminder that the original meaning of 'demon' was different. There was nothing horrid about it. On the contrary. The classical word could be translated as 'spirit' – the protective or determining spirit which gives and controls character.

The fact that each good and memorable golf course in Britain and America has its own essential eccentricity can be an important factor in gamesmanship. Possibly the most startling *daemon* courses occur in the United States, at any rate the proportion is high in those I know. A few of these examples may seem far fetched but I have the feeling that I was myself directly subjected to able gamesmanship in a way which some may find surprising.

The course which put me on the alert was in Kansas. I was lecturing at Kansas State University. All Englishmen who find themselves 1,500 miles from the nearest sea water feel particularly high and dry; but the hospitality was perfection, and I felt I had made some good new friends – until golf was arranged for me next morning. Talking about my game the night before, I had told the Lecturer in Italian Renaissance Architecture that I would like to play, although I was suffering at the moment from a serious tendency to hook.

'Good,' he said at once. 'I should be lecturing tomorrow morning but my student is sick. Let's play.'

No discussion as to which course – and in fact the one chosen for me was built round the sides of a conical hill which was played clockwise. With my hook, every ball I drove went bouncing down the slope into what seemed to be almost a different geological formation.

Chance, the reader may think: but what of this example of what I can only call DCmanship?

My hosts were distinguished members respectively of the C.I.A. and the *Washington Post*. I was longing, as always in America, for exercise. Burning Tree was suggested – which attracted me because I knew that the then President, Eisenhower, sometimes played there. I was putting well for some reason; and one thing about

America is that one can take one's time on the greens. On the 8th green I looked up. My opponents were talking. They sounded fidgety.

'Sorry,' they said. 'Only –'

'Anything up?' I said.

'Only that we think the President's here.'

'Oh yes?'

'Did you hear that plane 20 minutes ago? It's best to *keep going*, you know? On we get.'

He made a sweeping forward motion with his hand.

'He likes to do the course at some speed, you know?'

'Naturally.'

'Those two fellows ahead – probably got guns.'

In spite of all my experience, my game showed a hairline fracture, and I had to admit I was outgambited when I read next morning that the President was in Palm Springs. It put me on my guard for the future. 'Don't slice here, my friend,' said my opponent at Paradise Valley. This was one of those oasis courses, a sudden green place in the middle of the Arizona desert.

'Why, particularly?' I said, non-committally.

'You might find your ball in a nest of side-winders.'

I smiled, but there *were* snakes and I *had* seen a caddy with his arm in a sling. How can one be sure? Even when I first tasted the beauties of Cypress Point, the oldest member of our four-ball – actually he had a white goatee beard – told me at an important hole, made still more beautiful by the sparkling of the Western sun on the Pacific, that 'this was where we could see the seals – and hear them too, at this time of year'.

'Rather sweet,' I said, thinking of my shot.

'Listen. At this time of year it's their sexual roar.'

OLD WORLD EQUIVALENTS

English and Scottish courses have their own *daemon*, but it is more of an elf, very often, or sprite. Both countries excel in settings of fabulous beauty – ideal conditions for missing the ball completely on the first tee, courses like Pine Valley, Emperor of the American East, Pine Valley the majestic, almost compelling the newcomer either to attempt ridiculously enormous shots, or pokey little prodding shots, from nervousness and a feeling of inferiority.* In Scotland there are famous hostile courses, like Carnoustie – Irish Portmarnock could be included here – which have this effect: or dramatically handsome courses like Newcastle, County Down, bristling with quotes about the Mountains of Mourne. There is a new-boy-at-school feeling when we first play such courses. And has the Old Course, St Andrews, itself got a total gambit? For the new player there is a specialized form of hallowed turfmanship, world famous bunkers, sanctified burn, the immortal anxieties of the 17th and a general feeling that one is playing not only the course but history, behind the backs, turned indifferently towards us, of the ghosts of the most celebrated names in the game.

An interesting variation is the Killarney course,

* When I played Pine Valley I was at my worst and shortest, taking the 'Newcomer's Nine', standard for the first hole. But I had little chance. The famous captain of the Club, John Arthur Brown, then 70 and handicap four, received me. It is said that he was under the impression that I was Stephen Spender whose name of course stands high in literary circles in the U.S. He then entertained us, lunched us and played with me: and it is the custom, at Pine Valley, for other players to stand aside and allow the Captain and his guest to play through. Many couples had to stand aside for quite a time.

where the almost overpowering beauty of the rock and water type is softened by the acceptance of fishing as an O.K. alternative. It might be added here that the acceptance of fishing as a sideline grows daily, particularly in our Municipal Club, where the first tee is half under a gasometer and any visible stream is not quite perfect in content.

Muirfield has its own variation on the same theme. Here history is infrequently mentioned. Famous finishes over the last few holes in the Open are taken for granted. But one is faced with the nobility of pure golf in a Club where the ban on business talk is so complete that there is no professional's shop, and where the players are so single minded in the play that none of them have handicaps.*

Finally let us look at a few typical gambits peculiar to individual clubs. Many of these are haunted by an out-of-bounds reputation. 'Mind you don't slice at Lytham, pull at Hoylake, and above all in spite of that bunker on the left, don't slice on to the railway alongside the 4th at Woking.' This is a standard way of stiffening up the newcomer and being careful lest, because he doesn't know the dangers, he is going to be carefree. 'So flat,' they said of Royal Mid-Surrey. And who was J. H. Taylor to contradict them? Just the local pro., who covered the course with such a variety of traps and hummocks, slopes and pimples, that the stranger off line finds himself continually playing off some of the most discouraging angles in golf.

* Compare the fine gambit of the Portland Club where, in the bridge room 'they play no conventions'. 'Same with my car driving,' said Gattling to me, noticing my surprise at finding him in this Club. 'Let me take you home.' He was, I thought, a little 'on'.

Then there is Rye, whose resident *daemon* presides in summer, when the course is dry, when putts which are overhit on the 1st or the 5th green for instance scamper off the green on the other side,* or where some of the holes seem to be played on the crest of a smooth ridge, the back of a long animal – the 4th particularly, where one seems to be coaxing the ball along the backbone of an early cretaceous animal. Few can look, as they wander through the fossil reptile rooms of the

Natural History Museum, at the interminable backbone of *Diplodocus Carnegii*, without thinking of the fourth hole at Rye.

Or there are 'Beware' courses, like North Berwick, with those low stone walls.

'I should take a more lofted club if I were you,' I was told. 'If you hit that No. 5 a bit thin, it just won't carry the wall. Might do you an injury.'

'Well, actually I belong to Aldeburgh,' I used to reply. 'Those sleepers in the bunker at the short 4th. Simpson nearly lost an eye there.'

Sometimes the local put-offs can be unexpected. It is compulsory at Guadalmina, on the Costa del Sol, to have caddies, and to ask for them at their school, by the nearby hotel. On demand two are at once forthcoming. At the age of approximately nine, the ecstasy of being removed from the classroom is so great that joy and

---

* 'It'll be better in winter,' the gamesmen of Rye say to their visitors. In the winter, for some reason which has never yet been explained, the greens are even faster.

laughter and a desire to rush about cannot be confined. No need to say how putting-off this is to the player, who has to learn especial Spanish phrases to keep them in order. How different the atmosphere of Woking or Worplesdon, with their melancholy Autumn beauty. I think it was on the water hole at Worpers, last time I played there, that Darwin asked me, as I played my ball out from the trees into which my ball had unluckily rolled, not to 'hack about' too much.

'Why?' I said.'

'Middlewick's ashes,' he said, in a for him almost poetic sort of voice. 'They were scattered on this place.'

15
LAST WORDS

WHAT is the future of Golf Gamesmanship? It should and will, I believe, go in one direction or the other. First, it can intensify – and that is my hope – the essential squareness of golf. The retired major is the symbol of this school. The 'must wear a tie in the club-house' and, for ladies in the mixed bar, 'Off with your trousers and on with your skirts' – these are the watchwords, while on the course we insist, with gamesman's eye, on the strictness and rigour of the game. Younger people love it. By contrast others, including some older men are more for experiment. For them, startling bush shirts should be more startling, and in the summer, ladies should be dressed for sun-bathing. A multiple wave transistor could be carried so that music ranging from Spohr to The Spotties, could be switched on to form suitable background effect music to the match as it stands. The lines of development must obviously be kept sharply distinct, though they may be followed at the same club. There is some idea of keeping the Old and New Courses at Sunningdale distinct for this purpose.

NEWS FROM W.O.G.G.

There is little to report from Headquarters this year, except that our practice course at Moult Herring is now in full working order, and although the electric trolley car has no actual battery, it is possible to go through the motions of many simple ploys. We have at our disposal an area fully as big as a lawn tennis court, where we include a realistic temporary green, some useful *questionable lies* of the 'surely *this* is a rabbit scrape' kind – an innovation much appreciated by students; also some 'is this rough or not' grass for 'winter conditions'. We still have our dummy bar on the perimeter where we worked out correct way for

The dummy bar

winner to offer drink to loser (see p. 103). The bunker has grown greasy; but there are plenty for the 'at our Club we *remove* these stones. O.K.?' sequence.

Par gamesmanship for the course is 12. The record is 20. We have developed our instructions on how and when to instruct, especially aiming our teaching points for use against young men who have had dominating fathers. I remember that Odoreida never had any doubt about how to counter that one. Before opponent was half-way through the sentence 'do you mind if I tell you something?' Odoreida would wheeze out a 'Let's keep that particular sort of nonsense for after the game, shall we?' and shut his tiny mouth with a snap.

The Gold Gamesman of 1968 is, of course, de Vicenzo, who, by unpremeditated and unconscious gamesmanship, won the Masters though listed as second and actually tying for first place.

Golf Gameswoman of the year is Miss Penelope Burrows, who won the girls' championship at Liphook by a pretty variation on hat play. Although it is true that Miss Burrows (at the age of 18) was birdying, in this competition, such grimly difficult 4 holes as the 13th, her final success was judged to be due to the fact that after hitting every wood and long iron shot her beret fell off. Congratulations to Penelope and to her Aunt, Mrs Wilson (12) wife of our distinguished illustrator. The circle of girl golfers who chanted 'Keep it in the family' when our choice was made known is small and quite untypical.

Congratulations to E. Maudesley Hill for adding 25 specimens to his already large collection of peg tees. These have been amassed by Naval Lieutenant Hill from tees actually used by winners of club championships over the last 20 years and indeed there is a shelf of tees used by Ryder Cup players and a special set discarded or dropped by amateurs playing in the Wentworth Foursomes. Hill has perfected a common sense but effective method of mounting these tees.

A BAD HABIT

There is a growing habit, among unaffiliated gamesmen, of pointlessly sticking 'manship' on to the ends of words, in quite unsuitable contexts (as in the witless 'Central Heatmanship' of a fuel advertisement, to mention one among many score). This has caused universal annoyance among gamesmen and lifemen, from

San Diego to Upsala (the brilliant subtlety of Swedish lifemanship is proverbial). Moreover such actions have adulterated our message, and blurred the fine lines of the manship philosophy. It is true that not infrequently, natural lifemen, not on our executive com-

The Golf Gamesmanship Trophy

mittee, have invented, usually with graceful acknowledgement, a truly valuable contribution, such as the 'brinkmanship' of Adlai Stevenson, for which all of us are grateful. But among ourselves new manship words have to pass the most rigorous scrutiny before they are accepted. We are preparing our *Index Purgatorius* of allowed words and phrases – in the present volume, for instance, only three additions have been made, and two at least of these now look to me ephemeral and may soon be discarded.

1 Hallowed Turfmanship
2 On with the Motleyship
3 Top Playmanship

AVE ATQUE VALE

I have the lifeman's taste for Latin phrases which he not quite fully understands. But hail to the new generation of young gamesmen whose support, if and when I get it, is my pleasure. Op. 1. of my sequence was published in 1947. Gamesmanship, therefore, has now come of age. It is right, and I am glad, to leave it (with a touch of regret) in the hands of my successors as long as they refer to me for a final decision.

SACERDOS DUX VATES
PARENS ET CONJUX

INDEX

MORE ABOUT PENGUINS

Penguinews, which appears every month, contains details of all the new books issued by Penguins as they are published. From time to time it is supplemented by *Penguins in Print*, which is a complete list of all available books published by Penguins. (There are well over three thousand of these.)

A specimen copy of *Penguinews* will be sent to you free on request, and you can become a subscriber for the price of the postage. For a year's issues (including the complete lists) please send 30p if you live in the United Kingdom, or 60p if you live elsewhere. Just write to Dept EP, Penguin Books Ltd, Harmondsworth, Middlesex, enclosing a cheque or postal order, and your name will be added to the mailing list.

Note: *Penguinews* and *Penguins in Print* are not available in the U.S.A. or Canada

GEORGE MIKES

HOW TO BE AN ALIEN

George Mikes says 'the English have no soul; they have the understatement instead'.

But they *do* have a sense of humour – they proved it by buying some three hundred thousand copies of a book that took them quietly and completely apart, a book that really took the Mikes out of them.

Also available

HOW TO UNITE NATIONS
ITALY FOR BEGINNERS
LITTLE CABBAGES
MORTAL PASSION
ÜBER ALLES

STEPHEN POTTER

THE THEORY AND PRACTICE OF GAMESMANSHIP

Why play the game, when you can play *and win*? Study the whole 'Art of Winning Games Without Actually Cheating'; teach yourself the most effective ploys and hampers for court, course, pitch, table, and board. And then go in ... and 'may the best man win!' He will.

THE SENSE OF HUMOUR

What is this 'English humour' which as soon as it is persuaded on to the slide under the microscope swims out of focus. Is there a connexion between humour and laughter, which a multitude of thinkers from Hobbes to Bergson and Freud have tried to explain? Or do they, as it were, run parallel – the grin of laughter, the poker face of humour?

In *The Sense of Humour* the founder and inventor of One-Upmanship has made his bid to trap the butterfly of humour and dissect it. His book is more than a history and analysis of the English species; it is a heart-stirring anthology of humour from Chaucer and Shakespeare to Dickens and H. G. Wells – the latter recalling his adolescent dreams of military conquest in which he had so often fought his foes to a standstill at dawn on the battlefields of Bromley.

In fact, of Stephen Potter and humour we might say what *The Isthmian Book of Croquet* once pronounced about an expert:

'To excel at croquet in Mr Willis's style you must be – a Mr Willis.'